Praise for *The Ownership Society*

'James Vitali seeks to reclaim the word "bourgeois" by explaining that the values behind it (ownership, thrift, responsibility) are exactly what Britain needs more of. Britain works best when people have a stake in it. When families save. When people own things, look after them, and want to pass them on to the next generation. When citizens feel responsibility for their communities, not just demanding entitlement from the state.

In *The Ownership Society*, James Vitali argues that prosperity is not just about clever policies or clever politicians. It rests on deeper foundations: ownership, responsibility, thrift, family and belonging. These are the values of today's Conservatives: we call them common sense. And it's encouraging to see a new generation of Conservatives making the case for them again.'

Kemi Badenoch, Leader of the Conservative Party

'James Vitali's reflections on ownership, and the moral underpinnings of public policy, are not only an impressive contribution to the dying art of true political economy but he has also produced a workable manifesto for a radical reforming government of the right.'

David Goodhart, author of
The Road to Somewhere and *The Care Dilemma*

'James Vitali has diagnosed the twin ills of a fractured social order and a dysfunctional political economy with rare skill and insight. His prescriptions for how we can heal Britain are compelling. This book confirms that the most interesting ideas in British politics are Conservative and that James Vitali is one of the most impressive thinkers emerging in our country today.'

Michael Gove, editor of *The Spectator*

'Beautifully written, elegiac and inspirational: an appeal to the past and a celebration of the enormous benefits that private ownership – and the values it induces in us, responsibility, trust and generosity – can bring to the modern world. Vitali reminds us that politics is a moral project. His book could not be more timely or more necessary.'

Danny Kruger, Reform UK MP for East Wiltshire

'When politicians in this country have failed, it's so often because they've failed to understand what made this country so successful in the first place. This book is an invaluable contribution to the debate about where Britain's success has come from, how and why we've abandoned that social model, and what we can do moving forward to recapture it.'

Katie Lam, Conservative MP for the Weald of Kent

'James Vitali is one of the brightest young thinkers in this country, and his book is fizzing with ideas about how to put Britain back on track.'

Nick Timothy, Shadow Justice Secretary

The Ownership Society

The Ownership Society

How Bourgeois Values Can Save Britain

James Vitali

polity

First published in 2026 by Polity Press Ltd.

Polity Press Ltd.
65 Bridge Street
Cambridge CB2 1UR, UK

Polity Press Ltd.
111 River Street
Hoboken, NJ 07030, USA

ISBN-13: 978-1-5095-6952-6
ISBN-13: 978-1-5095-6953-3(pb)

A catalogue record for this book is available from the British Library.

Library of Congress Control Number: 2026934274

Typeset in 11.5 on 14pt Adobe Garamond
by Cheshire Typesetting Ltd, Cuddington, Cheshire
Printed and bound in Great Britain by Ashford Colour Ltd

For further information on Polity, visit our website:
politybooks.com

For my parents

Contents

Preface

Cynics say that to be a conservative, one needs to have something to lose. But I think it is truer to say that to be a conservative, one must have something to *conserve* – something of value that one wishes to protect and pass on. In this, conservatism is simultaneously noble and commonsensical: noble because it is committed to purposes higher than mere self-gratification; commonsensical, because this impulse is held by most people: most of us *do* have something we wish to conserve.

What I want to conserve is a way of life that used to be enjoyed by great swathes of the British public, but which is now under threat. It is a way of life defined by stable families and strong communities, by personal responsibility, trust and the opportunity for all to enjoy the fruits of their hard work. This is not an ostentatious or conspicuous existence. But it has an everyday heroism contained within it, and our free and prosperous society has long depended on a critical mass of people sharing in its spirit.

My view is the product of the instincts I learnt in childhood. I was raised in a village called Marnhull in Dorset's Blackmore Vale. It is a beautiful place, surrounded by rolling hills and well-maintained farmland. There is an architectural cohesiveness to the built environment too, its shop buildings and homes having been constructed to stand the test of time and reflect the place they were erected in.

Most people still know one another personally in Marnhull, often through the village's institutions and associations. It has several good primary schools and nearby secondary schools, vibrant sports clubs, excellent pubs and shops, and a number of churches, the largest of which, St Gregory's, sits at the top of the hill and dominates the surrounding landscape. It also has a strong sense of its own history, burnished by its close association with the novelist and poet Thomas Hardy, and the memorialisation of the many parishioners who served and died in the First and Second World Wars.

It is a trusting place. Voluntarism is widespread – from parents taking reading classes to retirees preparing the sports pitches. A local farmer – Mr Mogridge – maintains people's hedgerows; he takes donations but never solicits them. A lady purchases discounted bread from a local shop and delivers it personally to households which she knows might need it. People can rely on each other, and that reliability is its own source of self-sufficiency.

Most importantly, it is a community of *owners*. This is true in a narrow sense: most people live in homes of their own. But it is also true in a deeper sense. Marnhull is *owned* by its people in the sense that they feel personally responsible for conserving this precious place and passing it on to the next generation.

To some this probably sounds rather parochial, divorced from greater questions about building a more prosperous future for the country as a whole. But it is not. The viability of the way of life I have described is essential to our nation's prosperity. It is not upon the *grand projet*, nor the utopian design, that durable and broad-based affluence is built, but upon the values of personal responsibility, social obligation and ownership which are invariably taught in the context of community.

These values used to be pervasive in British society too. In fact, their pervasiveness was their strength and acted as a galvanising force among our people. They gave each a sense of stake, both in wider social and economic contexts and more local ones. If Marnhull is a neighbourhood of owners, Britain was a society of them.

But not anymore. Our politics has shifted towards the big and the impersonal and away from the everyday and the proximate. It values the grand and the designed over the human and the inherited. It prefers, in Alexis de Tocqueville's words, to *use* people to achieve great things, rather than to cultivate *great people*. We have ceased to encourage personal ownership in the broadest sense: the idea that every person and their decisions matter.

I believe our economic malaise stems from the decline of this ethic. People flourish when they are given the opportunity to take responsibility: when they are free to *choose* to do good. They do so best when they live within a community of tangible human relationships and mutual obligations. And when people are able to flourish, this is reflected in the vitality of the economy. That our economy has totally stagnated is a symptom of the reduced opportunities for human flourishing in Britain today.

I believe we're losing something precious. But I reject the view that this must be the case. The *Ownership Society* I believe in is not some nostalgic vision of a place lost to time. It remains a concrete reality for many, especially in towns and villages where social life continues to be defined by the depth of human relationships. We're not starting from scratch: this is a life we can cultivate and grow.

My reason for writing is that, by setting out the values that conservatives ought to promote in explicit and moral terms, I believe we have a better chance of restoring them. But this is a project that will require a complete divergence from the approach of recent governments to the challenges of our time. It demands a positive assertion of a particular way of life – *our* way of life – as more desirable in this place and in this society than other ones: it is not neutral or impartial about what the good life looks like, and it is not apologetic in trying to bring that vision about. It insists that policymaking be seen not merely as a technical exercise, but a cultural one too, in which the object is to foster a certain set of moral values. And it necessitates that responsibility, choice and agency are pushed back downwards, away from the state and towards individuals and the families and communities they belong to.

I believe I am articulating the conservatism of a new generation, one that is desperate for a sense of stake and belonging which for too long has been denied to them. It is a conservatism of those who feel disenfranchised from national life, but who want to do something about it: who possess a real desire to take ownership – for themselves, for their loved ones, for their communities. Channelling that desire is the surest way out of our current social and economic malaise.

Introduction: Poisoned Wells

It is the precept of ethical and humane behaviour, no less than of political wisdom, to adapt economic policy to man, not man to economic policy.[1] – Wilhelm Röpke

If old truths are to retain their hold on men's minds, they must be restated in the language and concepts of successive generations. What at one time are their most effective expressions gradually become so worn with use that they cease to carry definite meaning.[2] – Friedrich Hayek

The Machine

In 1949, Bill Phillips was invited to speak at a seminar at the London School of Economics. The subject of his presentation was a remarkable contraption that he had built in his garage in south London: the Monetary National Income Analogue Computer ('MONIAC'), or the 'Phillips Machine' for short. It stood about two metres tall and consisted of a labyrinthine network of chambers, sluice gates and columns.

MONIAC was designed to allow a trained technician to model the workings of the macroeconomy using the flow of water as national income. With the push of a button or the pull of a lever, a technician could manipulate the water around the machine and into different liquid tanks, which stood for things like 'consumption' or 'government spending' (you can still see a working Phillips Machine at the Science Museum in London, or at the University of Cambridge).[3]

Phillips is probably better known now for the 'Phillips curve': his model of the relationship between unemployment and inflation. But in some ways the impression his MONIAC machine has had on the political and economic thinking of this country has been vastly more pronounced. This is not as outlandish as it sounds: there is, in fact, a research methodology called 'hydraulic macroeconomics', dedicated to conceptualising the economy as if it operated like a Phillips Machine. The public, too, has come to understand the economy as a vast machine. Perhaps it presents itself more like an engine or a generator, with various valves and instruments, buttons and levers, inputs and outputs. But we talk about the economy as an artifice, a mechanical construction best operated or managed by a technician or an engineer – some intelligent mind capable of design and control. We speak of it as running 'hot' or 'cold', of politicians 'fixing' it when it breaks, of 'pump-priming' with fiscal stimulus.

Along the side of this vast imagined machine, we envisage a dashboard of various indicators, displaying the levels of inputs like labour, capital and credit, along with the factors that affect the machine's functioning, like inflation. At the bottom of the dashboard is a gauge that attempts to aggregate these factors into a single measure of the machine's operational output – gross domestic product (GDP) – which has become not simply a measure but the principal target of policy and the central focus of public discourse. The machine is built and operated by the engineer; its basic purpose is to sustain consumption, which in turn perpetually powers the machine.

This conceptualisation of the economy is accompanied by a certain understanding of how to create economic growth. Economists and public figures advance various theories about how to control the machine – what 'dials to turn' or 'buttons to press' – in order to improve that GDP measure. Some say that we need to pull the investment lever, others that we need to turn down the government expenditure dial, or to dial up more demand, or remove some of the regulators within the circuitry.

These theories fit into different camps or schools of thought labelled 'developmental' or 'neokeynesian' or 'modern supply-side'. But they all share a common assumption: that our underlying problems, in the words of Labour minister and economist Torsten Bell, 'are economic rather than cultural', and that, so long as the engineers pull the correct levers, the machine's output will improve.[4] Economics, as Paul Krugman once put it, holds forth the promise of ease and simplicity: 'of pushing a button to solve a problem'.[5] Growth, therefore, is a question of 'technique' – the consequence of a well-designed government 'mission', argues Mariana Mazzucato, much like putting a man on the moon.[6] Economic growth is a 'lever' to be 'pulled', Sir Keir Starmer said before entering office in 2024. 'Technology' and a 'strategic state', argues the Tony Blair Institute, 'is the only solution that can lift the UK out of its current crisis'.[7]

Yet despite all this – despite a myriad of different politicians and technicians positing different sequences of button-pressing – the British economy remains utterly stagnant. Per capita incomes have essentially not grown at all for twenty years. What could explain this? Many button-pressers presume that such stagnation can be traced back to a particular moment in our recent economic history. The pandemic accounts for the nosedive in public sector productivity and the surge in economic inactivity, some say, or the Great Financial Crisis explains why the regulatory apparatus has expanded to such a stifling extent or why investment has dried up.

But these are deceptions – illusions that comfort us by allowing us to pretend that our economic troubles can be attributed to a singular cause with a simple button-pressing remedy. The truth is that our economic fragility is not only more chronic than this, but of a qualitatively different nature. Indeed, the economy's unresponsiveness to tinkering suggests that the basic problems with our economy might not be of a technical nature at all: that our economic malaise might in some way be the product of a corresponding *cultural-moral* malaise in society; and that low economic growth is not therefore a failure of *engineering*, but the by-product of a society in ill health.

If all of this is true, then it follows that a lasting solution to our economic woes will not be found in the domain of technical economics or social science, but in that of moral and political philosophy – in an appreciation of how economic orders sustain certain types of society, and in turn how economies depend on certain external props and supports. The nature of those supports, and their erosion in Britain over a prolonged period, is the subject of this book.

Moral and Sociological Foundations

Here is an alternative metaphor. Imagine instead that our economy is a vast oak tree. Its thick trunk rises from the ground, from which branches reach in every direction. When everything is healthy, new shoots appear, leaves flourish, and the whole structure remains robust enough to withstand the elements. Yet beneath the surface lies a network of roots, hidden from sight, through which the tree receives nourishment and stability. Without them, the branches would fail to grow and the trunk itself would begin to wobble. If the tree is the economy, then its roots are the cultural values and moral principles that sustain it. We don't see these values in the same way that we see macroeconomic statistics, nor in the same way that we experience transacting with one another. But we certainly feel the effects when they're not there.

The way we have come to think about the economy has led us to forget the importance of these roots, and in so doing, we have inadvertently damaged them. We focus on repairing broken branches and pruning back the leaves, but we neglect the source of the tree's vitality. The result is an economy that can be made to look healthy for brief moments in time – or from a few select angles – but whose underlying structure is increasingly fragile.

For the true sources of our prosperity are not in the first instance technical, but moral and sociological in nature. They constitute a distinct set of values and a corresponding social structure that underpin the attitudes and behaviours of the public. Those values are concerned first and foremost not with consumption or the satisfaction of the individual as an *economic* actor, but with his or her flourishing as a human person, imbued with intrinsic worth. And it is human flourishing which generates the conditions for a healthy economy; it is the cultural foundations of our economic order that enable it to function properly.

What are these values? They are not the products of pure reasoning, nor did they emerge out of thin air at some specific point in time. But they are by no means arbitrary. They are a hard-won inheritance, a 'tradition' passed on to us by those who came before – the sedimentation, as Edmund Burke put it, left from the 'peculiar circumstances, occasions, tempers, dispositions, and moral, civil and social habitudes of a people, which disclose themselves only in a long space of time'.[8] Economic orders do not create these moral foundations; they presuppose them.[9]

In Britain, those foundations have historically rested on a worldview that treats individuals as ends in themselves – not as abstract economic units, but as moral *persons* who are embedded in families and communities, and who discover ultimate meaning in a sphere beyond economics. In this 'personalist' worldview, our capacity to flourish depends upon our freedom to choose right over wrong; politics begins with individual people embedded in their communities, and seeks to build structures and institutions around them.

The values associated with this outlook find practical expression in the idea of ownership. In a purely mechanical view of the economy, ownership means little more than a legal arrangement. But there is a different, *moral* conception of ownership too, and it is one that constitutes the very essence of our way of life. Ownership, in this sense, is what enables us to understand actions and their consequences – what makes tangible the ideas of moral culpability and justice; what underpins our intuitions about fairness and merit.

Ownership – 'to own' – refers to the propensity to take *responsibility* for something. We teach people to 'own up' when they make a mistake, by which we mean to bear the consequences of their decisions. Ownership is the concept that enables our society to isolate the moral agent within the myriad of social relationships and causal influences that make up human existence. It is the basis upon which we assign moral accountability, distinguish between criminal and victim, apportion praise and blame.[10] And it provides a means of growth and self-realisation; a means by which we can express our personality and character. In other words, it helps bind rights and responsibilities together – and so makes it possible for a society to be both free and virtuous.[11]

For centuries, this ethical system has been seen as distinctively *English* – the bourgeois prejudices of a 'nation of shopkeepers', as Napoleon apocryphally put it. Usually, this is meant disparagingly – as if a system built upon the values of ownership was narrow-minded and opposed to greatness. But it was these values that made our country great. Ownership breathed life into our economy. It aligned choice, risk and responsibility to individuals and their immediate communities, rather than to abstract systems or distant authorities. In so doing, it helped to sustain a social order in which economic freedom was intelligible, responsibility was an opportunity and prosperity was the natural by-product of a people given the space to flourish.

Disownership, Disorientation, Dislocation

Over time, however, these moral foundations have been weakened. Our culture of ownership has largely been replaced by a new worldview based upon totally different assumptions about freedom, responsibility and the economy. This view, *liberal rationalism*, has come to completely reshape our political and economic thought.

In many ways, liberal rationalism represents the defective ideology that early liberal writers warned about. It is a variant of liberalism that combines an exaltation of individual freedom, an absolute faith in human reason, and a conception of all socio-economic problems as technical challenges that reason alone can solve. This is the liberalism of the Phillips Machine – the liberalism of economic management emptied of any regard for the moral habits, cultural norms and relationships of the people who participate in it. In this view, culture is less a precondition of economic life than a constraint from which individuals ought to be liberated; moral and ethical considerations are hindrances – sand in the gears of the machine; *ownership* and the responsibilities it entails are a burden to be lifted.

This, however, is a deeply hubristic outlook, which in its complacency about what enables the free economy to function has in fact destroyed the basic conditions required for both freedom and prosperity. As this worldview has pervaded our society, the ethic of ownership has correspondingly weakened, and a great degeneration has occurred.

We see this degeneration materially, as fewer young people own homes, and fewer households own a stake in British businesses. The sturdy base of owners that once anchored our society has been thinned out.

But the decline of ownership is not just about bricks and mortar or company shares. It is visible in the fact that people are no longer personally responsible for a great many things in their lives. It can be identified in the rising levels of debt we are passing on to future generations, which now amounts to more than the entire economy. It can be seen in the balance between consumption, saving and investment, as we live for today but pass on crumbling infrastructure to tomorrow. It can be detected in the falling birth rate, as couples worry about the burdens and loss of liberty which parenthood implies.

It can be found in the preference for security over risk-taking, and in the attenuation of enterprise and innovation. It is behind the apparent preference among younger people for stable jobs in big bureaucracies over riskier forms of employment in private economy. And it is more pervasive still, affecting our views of criminal justice and the legitimacy of the distribution of wealth through society.

More concretely, we see this degeneration both in private economic trends and in the unchecked expansion of the state. Firstly, in a world in which people are taught that their economic freedoms are absolute and not constrained by corresponding responsibilities, selfish and extractive forms of exchange have proliferated. Financial services are increasingly defined by practices which are more akin to 'get rich quick' schemes than genuine attempts to attract investment to the parts of the economy that most need it. The community-oriented property holder has been replaced by the housing estate 'fleeceholder', who squeezes residents for as much money as possible. Water companies pay huge dividends and salaries while their infrastructure crumbles. Without a guiding sense of moral obligation, the private economy becomes increasingly brutish, too.

Simultaneously, we have abnegated a whole range of responsibilities in the personal realm, passing them up to the impersonal structures of the state. Today, the state is the provider of first resort for a range of social needs, and a regulator of the interactions between individuals and businesses. It is an active and expansive redistributor of wealth through taxation: as of 2025, almost fifty pence in every pound we generate is pumped into the state to secure our health, care for our loved ones or make provision for our retirement. The majority of British households are now net-dependent on the state, in that they receive more in state benefits than they pay in taxes. The state is an employer, directly or indirectly, of almost a third of Britain's workforce.

Our freedoms have been managed away too. The consequence of ceding our responsibilities to the state has been the mass infantilisation of the public, as our vastly overpowered state directs the economy on our behalf and treats citizens as the means to its own ends. We can now talk again of 'state ownership' – not in the older sense of its tangible ownership of assets, but in the wider sense that the state has assumed responsibility for a whole range of activities that previously were undertaken by individuals, families and communities.

Thus, our politics has been turned on its head. Now, it starts at the abstract, at the aggregate, at scale. It is man that must now be adapted to policy, not policy to man. We have moved from the personalist society to the depersonalised society, in which the individual moral agent finds himself lost in structures designed by a distant architect. Ultimately, our economy has lost the capacity to prosper, because we have forgotten how humans flourish.

And the uncomfortable truth is that, although these developments have been cheered on and accelerated by the statists and social democrats, those people who are ostensibly committed to freedom and the market have been their handmaidens. It is Conservatives who have let ownership (in both its narrow and broad senses) dwindle over the last few decades: who have allowed the state to take on ever-greater responsibility for an ever-growing list of social functions that used to be performed at the level of the family or the proximate community, and who have most conspicuously failed to articulate that a free economy based on diffuse ownership is not valuable simply because it provides for our material wants, but because it is connected to a much broader universe of moral values. All of this has happened because Conservatives in government have forgotten their moral convictions and made common cause with liberal rationalists.

Conservatism as Restoration

Economists and politicians tend to cite low investment, high taxes or low productivity as the issues blighting our economy. But in truth these are symptoms of a more serious, deeper-rooted disorder: our society today is unable to provide the basic conditions for humans to flourish. It is reducing the opportunities for people to exercise moral responsibility, shrinking the space for creativity and spontaneity, and leaving those communal sources of belonging, identity and social support to atrophy. Why support low taxes if the government is supposed to provide for all your wants and needs? Why invest for the future if all you are encouraged to do is maximise your consumption today? Why be industrious or enterprising without a family to share the proceeds with?

Our economic theories have come to 'reckon without man' – that is, without regard for his moral and spiritual needs, his dual nature as both subjective individual and member of genuine communities, and his dignity as a moral agent.[12] The inevitable result has been that all those other values which branched off from the vine of personalism have in turn withered too – values like responsibility and freedom, industry, self-sufficiency, all of which were essential to the healthiness of the economy.

A political economy which fails to provide for the moral development of the people cannot long subsist. We need to plug our economy back into the moral matrix from which it derives its energy and strength. We need to restore the human individual as a moral person with responsibility for their actions, and repair the communities in which that responsibility and sense of social obligation can be learned. And we urgently need to replenish the moral and ethical reserves that used to constitute the animus of our way of life. Most importantly, we must elevate and diffuse personal ownership and the values it embodies, and in so doing shift the centre of gravity in our society back down towards the local and the individual.

The arguments that follow in this book might appear at times focused on the realm of the individual person, and at other times that of the community; sometimes it will appear to make common ground with liberalism, sometimes with something closer to the school of thought which has come to be called 'post-liberalism'. But in this, it is simply advancing the *personalist* case, and a worldview that conservatives have held since at least Burke: that human nature is composite, that we require both recognition as individuals and a sense of belonging in communities to thrive, and that freedom might be 'a very good horse to ride', as the poet Matthew Arnold once put it, 'but to ride somewhere'.[13]

In fact, the case to be made here is decidedly *not* a liberal one. It is premised on the view that contemporary liberalism is largely the problem to be solved, and that it has unwittingly assisted the statism which characterises our politics today. It concurs with those critics of liberalism who contend that it is largely degenerative in its contemporary manifestations, and it believes strongly in the necessity of rebuilding those moral foundations of the free economy which liberals are either ignorant of or have proactively undermined. It agrees that liberalism has utterly failed for decades to provide for the non-individualistic aspects of people's lives.

But nor is my case post-liberal. It maintains, alongside the liberal view, that the good life can only truly subsist in a context of freedom, and that the response to liberalism's shortcomings cannot be to shrink the sphere of moral agency for the individual. It values a great many of the things that liberalism values – the emphasis on personal responsibility and the belief that all humans should be afforded the opportunity to be moral actors in their own right – but it believes that liberalism in practice has been a poor vehicle for promoting them.

My case is *conservative, with a small 'c'*.[14] It wishes to preserve and perpetuate a cultural inheritance that positively shapes and moulds people's dispositions and values. It seeks to identify those moral and cultural supports which previously undergirded our way of life but which have been neglected. It understands those supports to be a *tradition* – a product not of design but historical experience peculiar to our national context. Yet it believes that passive transmission will no longer be sufficient today, because the damage done to that inheritance has been so extensive and acute.

The task at hand demands a different type of conservatism – one that repudiates the direction of travel of all governments in recent decades. For many, 'natural' conservatism is dispositional, sceptical, non-ideological. It shies away from statements of principle, save that, while change is necessary, it should be moderated and controlled. It 'is to prefer', in the words of Michael Oakeshott, 'the familiar to the unknown . . . the tried to the untried, fact to mystery, the actual to the possible, the limited to the unbounded, the near to the distant, the sufficient to the superabundant, the convenient to the perfect, present laughter to utopian bliss'.[15]

But what happens when the familiar is rotting? When 'the actual' is eroding our society's consensus on basic moral issues? When seeking convenience risks furthering our social and economic malaise? In such moments, that natural, dispositional variant of the creed will be found to be totally inadequate for the challenge to which conservatives in all eras must rise: that of conserving forms of social and political order that promote flourishing.

We now find ourselves in precisely this sort of political moment; a moment when 'the fibres of society have been rudely torn apart, when deleterious revolutionary principles ride high, and restoration, not preservation, is the order of the day'. In such circumstances, conservatives must remember that we are committed to conserving 'not simply whatever happened to be the established conditions of a few years or a few decades' but the consensus of our 'civilization', a moral inheritance forged over generations.[16] In a society that has forgotten what that inheritance looks like, conservatives must state what they value in confident, principled language. They must answer, in other words, the question posed by Disraeli in his novel *Coningsby*, namely: 'what will you conserve?'[17]

The truly conservative mission today must be *restoration*: the restoration of an order that is being lost but which can be recovered – not the passive acceptance of present social arrangements. Those sentiments and values which were the 'by-products' of an inherited political order must now be the explicit 'products' of conservative policy.[18] No doubt some will throw up their arms and claim that we cannot 'put the clock back', and must trudge, one foot in front of the other, down the self-destructive path we are currently set on as a society. In responding to this fatalism, we should remember the counsel of C. S. Lewis: of course you can put the clock back, and 'if the clock is wrong it is often a sensible thing to do'. Progress, as Lewis said, 'means getting nearer to the place where you want to be'; if you are on the wrong road, 'progress means doing an about-turn and walking back to the right road'.[19]

Adopting such a principled conservatism will undoubtedly feel uncomfortable to many on the British right who believe the free market justifies itself, or who have been conditioned by the view that the free economy is value-neutral, and that this is a critical aspect of its appeal. Others, still, have argued that humans are largely divided into opposing psychological camps – 'thinkers' who are receptive to facts and logic, and 'feelers' who respond better to arguments about values – and that what our political debate needs is a strong dose of hard empirical reasoning, not appeals to moral principle.[20]

No doubt it does. But the presumed dichotomy between these ways of thinking is a false one. For as David Hume pointed out some three hundred years ago, 'reason alone can never produce any action': what gives rise to volition and motivates the will is our 'passions'. Reason is only ever the 'slave' of our passions, and it is our instinctive feelings and convictions that determine the ends we seek.[21] In other words: if we fail to make the principled case, if we fail to appeal to people's hearts as well as their heads, we will also fail to reverse the growth in the size of the state, the increase in worklessness, the deterioration of productivity, and, as the sum of those trends, the reduced capacity of people in this country to flourish.

Conservatism operates 'with the grain' of human nature – it naturally accords with our instinctive desire for an existence that provides for both individual distinction and social belonging, and it accords with our intuitive sense that humans are morally capable actors who ought to be given the *opportunity* to take responsibility for their lives. In this, it has a distinct advantage. But it suffers from a willingness, as one conservative once put it, 'to leave its view of life unexplained, its principles unstated', while liberals and socialists go about 'setting out their aims and ideals' fearlessly and untiringly.[22] In a context in which those supportive instincts are diminished, conservatism must break its silence and set out clearly what it believes and why.

For people to support the free economic system, they need to understand it on a principled level: they must reflexively comprehend why it is good and how it fits into a wider system of values. Conservatives must, therefore, first win a principled argument over the type of economy we aspire to, and what is necessary to sustain it. Only then can we deploy economic arguments about how to improve its operation.

We must also ditch the comforting idea that economic growth will solve our society's moral and cultural schisms. It is a notion endemic in liberal thought, and has induced so many on the right to recoil from participating in debates about values in favour of focusing on the everyday administrative business of running the economy, as if the two can be neatly separated. In fact, this is to get our current predicament precisely the wrong way around. It is cultural developments that have led to a larger state and a subdued private sector, and it is through restoring a culture supportive of work, enterprise and responsibility, that we will improve our shared economic prospects.

More than anything else, conservatives must strengthen the case for personal ownership, which has always served as a vital ethical prop for the free economic system, and the loss of which has permitted the economy and society more broadly to become disassociated from one another. This book attempts to do precisely that.

An Ownership Political Economy

The rest of the book is divided into seven chapters. Chapter one sets out a fuller diagnosis of our economic discontents. It considers the sociological and economic effects of that powerful cultural solvent in contemporary society – liberal rationalism. It shows how this solvent has eroded the external supports that our economic activity once relied upon, how it has contributed to a sociological transformation of society and precipitated the growth of the state, and how all of this is undermining our economic performance today.

Chapter two considers the proper role of the state in society. In a system founded upon personal ownership, responsibility and freedom, the state must inevitably have a smaller role – but conservatives have failed to identify that role effectively, and therefore lack solid grounds from which to respond to those who see it as the answer to everything. This chapter argues for a 'Cincinnatus state' that creates the conditions for personal ownership and self-sufficiency. An essential aspect of that task, the chapter will argue, will be rehabilitating those smaller forms of community which used to discharge functions that have since been assumed by the state.

In chapter three, I put forward the case for a vast diffusion of property ownership through British society. For too long, British policymakers have failed to meaningfully increase the number of property owners in this country, and have sought to compensate for this failing through wealth redistribution. This approach has weakened our social structure, diminished the values of ownership and harmed the economy. To address the situation, we need to adopt precisely the opposite strategy – to radically scale back redistribution through the tax system but dramatically increase the number of people owning forms of property.

Chapter four considers the context for that diffusion of ownership – the patterns of savings, consumption and investment, and the bearing of those patterns on future prosperity. For some time, our economic model has been primed towards sustaining and expanding present consumption. But this model has exacted a heavy price on British society – particularly the frayed relationship between generations and the loss of our propensity to save and fund the investment we desperately need.

In chapter five, I turn to the question of welfare. The tendency to see the state as responsible for solving every form of social problem has accelerated the development of dependency in British society and sapped the vigour of both those who pay into the system and those who benefit from it. I propose a conservative alternative, one based on reducing poverty by empowering individuals, families and communities to be more self-sufficient, and enlarging the space for moral agency rather than shrinking it. It will consider reforms to the provision of welfare, healthcare and social care in Britain.

Chapter six concerns the effects of immigration and multiculturalism. Mass levels of immigration and the absence of any coherent integration policy have diluted our collective sense that British citizenship comes with both rights *and* responsibilities – that citizens should properly be 'owners' of their country with a sense of investment in its future prospects. I argue for a less permissive approach to immigration, and a policy on education and citizenship that proactively strengthens our social structure, rather than weakens it.

In the final chapter, I bring together these moral and spiritual arguments into concrete proposals for government. This is not a technical policy book, and certain questions of policy design fall beyond its scope. But since my purpose here is to recover a set of principled arguments about the way our economy should be structured and organised, it falls to me to spell out what those principles specifically entail in practice today.

I advocate, in short, for *The Ownership Society* – for the most transformative repatriation of responsibility in our nation's history, and a programme to profoundly rebalance the relationship between individuals, families, civil society and the state in Britain. It will involve reducing considerably the role of government in our lives – not in the deeply careless manner that Conservative politicians have sought to do so in recent decades, but with a clear view of what the state is *for*, and proactive efforts to help civil society grow in the state's absence. Its material basis would be an extensive diffusion of property ownership, such that millions more British people would have the opportunity of a stake in our economy and society. It would see the government moving from sole provider of first resort to one source of provision within a far more pluralistic model of social support, alongside a systematic devolution of fiscal responsibility. It would demand a shift from our presentist, consumptionist economic model to one that prioritised long-term investment in our country's productive capacity. And it would require an end to mass immigration, as well as a national effort to promote societal cohesion and integration. The guiding rationale for this great endeavour is the return of the human person to the centre of policymaking, and the revitalisation of a culture that supports her or his flourishing.

Be under no illusions – the path I contend for represents a decisive change of course for our country, and an end to a consensus that has undergirded our politics not just for the last two or three decades, but in many ways since the Second World War. It would involve political bravery, public engagement and *risks* – risks that are inescapable if people are to have genuine control and responsibility in their own lives again. But its ambition is commensurate with the scale of the challenge we face in restoring our country. And its promise is a prosperous, confident and cohesive Britain, in which the opportunities to flourish are greatly multiplied.

Above all else, what follows is an impassioned defence of ownership and the values it incorporates. I believe profoundly that the proper end of all politics must be the moral development of the people who live in our society. I believe that this development can only occur in conditions of free choice. But freedom alone will never suffice. Freedom permits the possibility of doing good, but we do not do good simply by being free. This confusion about the nature of freedom in a good society is the basic defect of contemporary liberalism, and it explains why decisions taken on the basis of liberal principles have in many cases left our society less united, less dynamic and less spiritually *healthy*. For a free society to endure, it must also be a responsible one, for it is in taking responsibility for ourselves and for those around us that we grow as moral persons. And it is through being an *owner* that we learn the propensity to do just that.

1

Diagnosis

Today's rulers appear to be seeking to use men to achieve great things. I should like them to think a little more of creating great men, to attach less value to the work and more to the workman and never to fail to remember that a nation cannot remain strong for long when each individual man is weak, and that we have still not discovered a social formula, nor any political ruse, which can turn a nation of small-minded and flabby citizens into one that is full of energy.[1] – Alexis de Tocqueville

But what is liberty without wisdom and without virtue? It is the greatest of all possible evils; for it is folly, vice, and madness, without tuition or restraint. Those who know what virtuous liberty is cannot bear to see it disgraced by incapable heads, on account of their having high-sounding words in their mouths.[2] – Edmund Burke

Liberal Pathologies

British society today is marked by a curious paradox: it is simultaneously the freest and the most constrained it has ever been. We have more license to do or think or be whatever we want now than at any other historical epoch. We have greater choice as consumers than ever before. We have more absolute freedom over where we live and work, how and where we invest our capital, or what we do with our bodies, than at any other time in history.

Yet at the same time, the state is penetrating into the lives of its citizens to an unprecedented degree. Some thirty people a day are being arrested for offences related to social media posts.[3] Government regulation touches almost every aspect of our lives – from the precise layout of new homes to what counterterrorism measures a village hall needs to take. Government ministers wish to supervise whether or not children brush their teeth in the morning, and what they eat for breakfast. And all of this activity is supported by the biggest state bureaucracy – and the biggest peacetime tax burden – our country has ever seen.

How is it that we are somehow simultaneously more and less free? The answer lies in the fact that liberalism, the ideology that has dominated our politics for decades, is inherently self-destructive. In this, the deterioration of Britain's economy is tragic in the true sense of the word: liberalism's success has sown the seeds for its failure.

For defenders of the free economy, this can be difficult to grasp. Liberals who believe in competitive markets, individual choice and private property feel as if they are locked in a constant battle with those who wish to expand the size of the state, reduce the scope for choice and competition, and in so doing strangle the dynamism of the economy. It is therefore unsettling to recognise that the conditions for the expansion of the state, the diminution of freedom and the subsequent impairment of vital economic incentives were generated by the fervent application of liberal principles.

Some think the solution to our economic ailments is straightforward. The problem, so this line of thought goes, is low economic growth. And since historically we can prove a causal relationship between free market economies and durable growth, we simply need to introduce the requisite technical reforms to reduce the burden of regulatory interference or constrain the size of government, and economic performance will surely improve. Some have even argued that we can predict the rate of growth that will be achieved based on the size of the state within the economy; that an increase in the government's size by ten percentage points is associated with a 0.5 per cent lower annual growth rate, or that the size of the state is responsible for about a third of an economy's growth rate, and so on.[4] Who could possibly argue with such evidence! For those of such a view, defenders of the free economy need simply to demonstrate the empirical connection between free markets, free trade and growth, and corresponding policies and public support for them will follow.

Yet statist economic models have been thoroughly discredited by their dismal records in practice, and still people remain unpersuaded by the case for the free economy. Hoping, then, that the results of a free economy will *deliver* us a free economy is a non-starter. People do not *want* freer markets, even when they work as intended. Lower taxes and a smaller state are seen not as the upshot of a decent, moral conception of a good society, but as evidence of callousness or a lack of generosity or compassion. Attempts to reduce state intervention in markets are not seen as expanding the scope for human enterprise and initiative, but a dereliction of the state's duty to eliminate risk from our lives and provide for our economic security. In such a situation, merely preaching the efficiencies of the free economy and its relationship with output can only be woefully inadequate.

What is driving this situation? To answer this, we must focus not on the evidence for why free markets are economically judicious, however compelling it is, but on a *cultural* development that is undermining the legitimacy of the free economy and therefore our economic vitality too. A virus is attacking the very source of our prosperity: that is, the integration of our economy within a particular type of society, with a commitment to human flourishing and a firm sociological structure held together by the cement of shared moral values.

The Personalist Inheritance

Political worldviews can be understood through the metaphors they employ. Progressives tend to employ mechanical images to depict society and the economy, as if they were fashioned by human agents according to a design or on the basis of a 'social contract'. Conservatives tend to prefer organic metaphors of social orders, as comparable to a living being that develops not according to a particular set of designers but in response to the environment provided by a particular place or time.

In the case of our economy, the organic metaphor seems entirely more appropriate. Our country's economic arrangements – arrangements that have brought remarkable prosperity, lifted millions out of poverty, and historically did so in conformity with a distinctive way of life – were not the product of conscious design but the product of a complex historical development. They evolved spontaneously over time and emerged coterminously with a set of moral values that were peculiar to our own national circumstances. These values were intuitive and unthought, but they made sense of interactions for those participating in the economy.

Economic theory is oriented around a particular set of assumptions about how individuals will behave in the context of an economic exchange. What is often overlooked is the fact that the way individuals think about their interests is shaped by social contexts, where actions have a meaning and significance that is not narrowly economic. Adam Smith's famous analogy of the butcher and the baker is often employed to demonstrate that the basis of economic activity is pure self-interest. But as Smith himself knew, the interactions between the butcher and the baker and their customers do not occur in a vacuum. They make sense because they take place in a framework of expectations and values that precedes that economic interaction – a framework which emerges from society, rather than from the economy itself.[5]

That framework is the product of a common set of values that are moral rather than economic – they relate to how individuals should interact with one another, about legitimate political authority, about what it is to flourish and about how economic considerations fit within that broader moral scheme. An economic order, in other words, is not self-standing. It depends on and draws from the 'ethical reserves' of those who participate in it.[6]

In this country, the foundation of those moral values is a commitment to what might be called personalism – a worldview that holds the human individual to be imbued with an inalienable dignity, and therefore to be entitled without qualification to be treated as an end, never a means to some further end. It is a religiously inflected conception which has its roots in our shared Christian inheritance – the belief that the human person is 'the visible image of the invisible God' and is 'therefore by his very nature the subject of rights which no one may violate'.[7] Specifically, this worldview gets its moral force from the view that all humans possess a moral conscience, are responsible for their actions in this life, and will be held accountable for them in the next.

This belief, that humans have some special and irrevocable claim to special status as intrinsically valuable and morally responsible, does not emerge spontaneously in all human societies or as the inevitable product of rational intellectual inquiry. In fact, it is a historically peculiar conviction, and one that was nourished specifically by the biblical teaching that each and all of us is made in the image of God. As Tom Holland has argued so persuasively, '[T]he well-spring of humanist values lie not in reason, not in evidence-based thinking, but in history: the history of Christianity.'[8]

But the roots of the personalist worldview are not solely Christian. They are to be found too in a tradition which runs from classical antiquity through to certain strains of thought in the Enlightenment – traditions that hold that humans are possessed of free will, and that moral development occurs when individuals must choose freely between right and wrong. The Kantian categorical imperative – to 'act in such a way that you treat humanity, as much in your own person as in the person of every other, always at the same time as end and never merely as a means' – is a restatement of the same biblical teaching to treat others as you would wish to be treated.[9]

This attentiveness towards the individual person has very deep roots in English history, and was nourished by sociological peculiarities that distinguished it from other European countries for centuries. Even the English peasantry, Alan Macfarlane has argued, were defined by the emphasis they placed on the individual moral actor in a way that marked them out from other nations – an argument which accords fully with observations made by Alexis de Tocqueville in the nineteenth century and Montesquieu in the eighteenth.[10]

Personalism represents the 'joint inheritance' of these spiritual traditions. *And it is an inheritance* – the precious product of accumulated wisdom and experience that stretches generations; slow and difficult to create but easy to destroy. It is why so often thinkers have spoken of English or 'Anglican' liberties, rather than the more universal 'liberty of man'.[11]

Personalism locates the proper site for moral agency at the level of the individual because it asserts that free choice – *freedom* – is a prerequisite for goodness. The good act must be freely chosen, so it is only in a context of free choice that the moral development of a person can take place. And it demands a particular set of social and political arrangements. In the personalist view, a good society is one that aims at the *flourishing* of its inhabitants – not just their immediate pleasure but, as Aristotle understood it, their moral development, and their living of a 'good life' in which they can fulfil their potential as beings both individual and social. And this in turn requires that society creates the space in which individuals can exercise their moral agency.[12]

This gives the respect that personalism affords to freedom a particular, sceptical aspect. It does not see humans as perfectible, or believe their judgements will always be wise or judicious. It recognises that humans are fallible beings, but that if they are to exercise moral agency, they must be free to choose evil, as well as to choose good. This justification for freedom relates to the intrinsic moral status of humans *qua* human; it is the condition that enables humans to act morally.

All of this renders the free economy – one in which individuals and associations of individuals determine the direction of their economic activity, rather than themselves being directed by a superintending authority – as the only model compatible with personalism. The free economy represents the sole economic form based upon the 'spirit of initiative', in which humans might be treated as intrinsically valuable, and in so doing enabling their moral development.[13] It is best understood in relief to its opposite: the *coercive* economy, in which economic activity is determined by a controlling power according to some plan. This, then, is the chief difference between the free and the coercive economy; the former adapts economic policy to man, while the latter seeks to bend man to economic policy.[14] And so these systems represent not merely different techniques for the management of an economic machine, but divergent visions of morality.

None of this is to say that evil, coercion or injustice are not experienced in the free economy. But it is to say that true human flourishing is only possible in a society in which individual persons are free to choose between right and wrong. Liberty is 'constitutive' of our existence as moral beings, and the 'ability to sin', as Emmanuel Mounier put it, is 'essential to the full exercise of liberty'.[15] A coercive economy might be one in which people are bullied to give away all the fruits of their labour to others, or to dedicate their lives to caring for the vulnerable. But that would not make it a generous or compassionate society. The existence of coercion or injustice in a free economy only demonstrates the insufficiency of liberty to generate a good society by itself.

Of course, these moral principles distinguish the personalist ethic from socialism, which holds the conviction that society ought to be directed towards moral ends determined at the level of the state – a conviction which is irreconcilable with an ethic committed to the individual person as an end in themself. As Pope John Paul II put it,

> Socialism . . . maintains that the good of the individual can be realized without reference to his free choice, to the unique and exclusive responsibility which he exercises in the face of good or evil. Man is thus reduced to a series of social relationships, and the concept of the person as the autonomous subject of moral decision disappears, the very subject whose decisions build the social order.[16]

But the personalist ethic is to be distinguished from liberalism too. While the latter holds that freedom is the highest moral end, personalism affirms that it is merely a necessary condition for the more important object of flourishing. In fact, the personalist conception of human nature means that freedom alone can never suffice. Humans, personalism holds, are inherently dualistic; they require both distinction and solidarity – a conception of human nature that is to be found deep in our Christian and humanist inheritance. It can be found in Kant's notion of humankind's asocial sociability, our desire for both social solidarity and individual differentiation, as in the Christian belief that men and women have both a personal relationship with God as well as common membership in the community of the church.[17]

Personalism thus ascribes considerable value to the obligations that humans might incur as part of their membership to *communities*, by which I mean not just some thin notion of a local area, but as Robert Nisbet put it, 'all forms of relationship which are characterized by a high degree of personal intimacy, emotional depth, moral commitment, social cohesion, and continuity in time'.[18] Sociologists have sometimes called these forms of community that exist between the individual and the state 'mediating structures'.[19] But this is highly misleading. The significance of communities is not that they 'mediate' the relationship between individuals and government; their immeasurable value lies in the fact that they permit *unmediated*, personal relationships between human beings. And the most important, most personal form of community is the family, where we are schooled in the principles of moral responsibility.

Liberals can only see these obligations as an incursion of freedom, but for the personalist it is by acknowledging them that we develop our moral character. Indeed, it is through loving our family, with all the mutual obligations such love implies, that we learn to be obligated to our neighbours, to our country and to humankind itself. The liberal believes that a sense of obligation derives from man's universal capacity for reason. The personalist believes it is the product of love, and a love learned first in the proximate and intimate context of the family. 'It is in interrelationships on many levels that a person lives, and that society becomes personalised.'[20] 'The person only exists', wrote Mounier, 'towards others, it only knows itself in knowing others, only finds itself in being known by them.'[21]

Personalism's understanding of the individual also differs from that of liberalism ontologically. Liberalism considers the individual to be bounded by the material body and its possessions. But personalism acknowledges that an individual's family, their neighbourhood and their community are in some ways an extension of him- or herself. This attachment to others whom we experience as a part of ourselves is called *loyalty*, and that loyalty is not a superfluous addition to the individual personality, but an integral aspect of it.[22]

And so personalism emphasises that some equilibrium must be established between distinctiveness and group membership. As Arthur Schopenhauer put it, humans resemble the porcupine on a cold day who wishes to gather close to his fellows for warmth yet avoid being pricked by their quills. 'When the need for warmth once more brought them together, the drawback of the quills was repeated so that they were tossed between two evils, until they had discovered the proper distance from which they could best tolerate one another.'[23]

Ownership and the Bourgeois Ethic

The personalist moral settlement has historically translated into a specific set of views which we might call 'bourgeois'. They include the virtues of thrift and industry, personal enterprise and initiative, self-reliance, responsibility – for oneself and for those proximate – the veneration of the family, a firm conception of right and wrong, charity, a scepticism about the intellectual capacity of humans and their ability to transcend their basic condition, and a sense of the social obligations incurred to previous generations, as well as future ones.[24]

The most important of these values, however, is ownership. For those worldviews which are blind to the moral and ethical prerequisites of economic activity, ownership simply refers to the ability to alienate, dispose of or derive benefit from something of value. But this is not quite what I am talking about. Ownership is also a *moral* concept. It denotes the propensity to take responsibility – for ourselves, for our decisions and for those around us. It is the condition of having a 'stake', from which we derive both the possibility of future benefit, but also liability for future risk.

Ownership anchors social life at the level of the individual person, embedded in proximate forms of community. Some have argued that ownership has no necessary connection with the individual; that ownership exists on a 'spectrum' that runs all the way up to collective ownership.[25] And this may well be true if we are discussing the narrow, legal concept of ownership. But as a moral idea, ownership refers specifically to the individual, for it is in the sphere of individual conduct where moral decision-making is possible. It is dedicated to the concentration and crystallisation of moral responsibility, not its diffusion, for 'what everybody owns, nobody owns'.[26] And this connects ownership as a concept with the much broader moral framework of personalism. To be a moral agent in some way is to be an owner – to be responsible for your decisions, or to 'own' them.

Yet ownership has a social significance, too. It is the source of the vitality of our communities, and of the civic institutions that sit between individuals and political authority. This is the paradox of ownership – that diffuse personal ownership actually generates the sense of common cause and obligation that nourishes community. That sense of personal stake is what enables groups of people to avoid the 'tragedy of the commons', in which the community concern is the responsibility of all, but in practice becomes the responsibility of none. Durable communities require owners with a stake in their fortunes – with a sense that their community's health and condition is their *personal* responsibility. And they require that sense of ownership to be widely held.

And it is through ownership that our way of organising economic activity becomes morally legible too. It makes sense of economic freedom – in which individuals and associations of individuals direct their economic activity. It promotes entrepreneurship, enterprise and initiative. It gives a moral aspect to the thrift of the saver who provides for themselves and their loved ones and does not need to turn to the state. It inculcates a sense of the present's obligations to the past and future – obligations to conserve what has been built up, to invest in future prosperity, to not pass on debts and burdens to those yet to be born. It encourages voluntarism and community solidarity. And it teaches a healthy approach towards risk, one in which the risk-taker deserves the opportunities that come with deploying capital in the context of uncertainty, as well as the responsibility for bearing the costs of their actions if things go wrong.

'Bourgeois' is usually deployed as a term of contempt – to describe the parochial, prosaic values of the middle classes. But while these values might be 'unexciting', they have 'the immense advantage of being rather attainable by everyone'.[27] As such, they can have a stabilising effect: in being held by a critical mass of people, they can help to produce a particular sociological structure in society – one undergirded by a firm base of individual property owners, rooted in families and committed to their own self-sufficiency, punctuated by small forms of community and association which gained their weight and substance from the sense of stake of their members.

As the great sociologist Max Weber observed, this bourgeois moral settlement imbued the free economy with a 'spirit' – with an animating purpose, a distinctive mode of thought, a sense of 'calling' to those who participated in it.[28] And it was this spirit and its implications for the economy that constituted the wellspring of economic growth and thus prosperity. In its commitment to the sphere of individual decision-making, the bourgeois settlement promoted the fullest expression of human creativity and innovation. It esteemed the entrepreneur and the responsible risk-taker, the small enterprise, the *owner*. It venerated the family that provided for itself and made provisions for its future, and in this fostered a healthy sense that we all have obligations to those who have gone before and those who are yet to come. It also created a sense of *personal* social obligation – where addressing the concerns of the poor and the vulnerable was considered a direct commission of free men and women, not a task to be outsourced to someone else.

These values have roots deep in Britain's past. Until the 1960s, there was a scholarly consensus that they were a product of 'capitalism, industrialisation and urbanisation', but that view has come under sustained assault since then. The 'ethics and organisation' of its 'small towns and villages' marked English society as distinct from that of other European countries 'for a very long period' before the Industrial Revolution, the sociologist Alan Macfarlane contended.[29] According to Emmanuel Todd, the values of the small, self-sufficient and enterprising family 'in a sense expresses [the English] historical tradition', stretching back as far as 1250.[30]

Arguably, the high point for such values is to be found in the mid-nineteenth century. In his *Self-Help*, Samuel Smiles argued that 'the spirit of self-help is the root of all genuine growth in the individual' and 'the true source of national vigour and strength . . . Whatever is done for men or classes, to a certain extent takes away the stimulus and necessity of doing for themselves; and where men are subjected to over-guidance and over-government, the inevitable tendency is to render them comparatively helpless'.[31] Yet Smiles believed the spirit of personal responsibility to be an ancient and 'marked feature of the English character', and it was this ordinary, popular spirit, not simply the deeds of great men and women, which made England great:

> Though only the generals' names may be remembered in the history of any great campaign, it has been in a great measure through the individual valour and heroism of the privates that victories have been won. . . . Even the humblest person, who sets before his fellows an example of industry, sobriety, and upright honesty of purpose in life, has a present as well as a future influence upon the well-being of his country; for his life and character pass unconsciously into the lives of others, and propagate good example for all time to come.[32]

About a quarter of a million copies of *Self-Help* had been sold by Smiles's death in 1904. In their *The English Middle Classes*, Roy Lewis and Angus Maude contend that, by then, an 'age of guilt' was already beginning to sow seeds of doubt about the values

Smiles championed. But, their own book, written in 1949, was itself a paean to the ethic of ownership and the middle classes that championed it: the latter, Lewis and Maude argued, 'conserve and transmit' a values system which comprised the 'stored experience of the whole nation'. And it was this system that they thought provided the 'main barrier' against overbearing government and misrule.[33]

Even George Orwell recognised that these values had some deep relationship with the English character (though he certainly would not have described such values as 'bourgeois'). They manifested themselves, Orwell wrote, in a respect for liberty – not the 'economic liberty' of self-interest, but the liberty of the private sphere: the liberty 'to have a home of your own, to do what you like in your spare time, to choose your own amusements instead of having them chosen for you from above'. It was also, he argued, a trait of the English to balance this respect for liberty with a gentleness and 'common decency' towards others. He loathed those on the left and the right who, in their lack of obligation to others in the national 'family', resembled 'irresponsible uncles'. They were, for him, in some way *un-English*, defined in part by their 'severance from the common culture of the country'.[34]

British prosperity increased immensely in the period in which the ethic of ownership was in the ascendancy, and there is good reason to think that this was not incidental.[35] Yet growth was the by-product of a system based on personal ownership, not its *purpose*. And critically, these bourgeois values did not derive from the free economy itself; they were external to it – a spiritual and moral inheritance which the economy draws upon but cannot itself produce.[36]

If personalism is ultimately a matter of faith or belief, the bourgeois economic values it has supported have a more historical or 'traditional' legitimacy.[37] That is, they have created a presumption in favour of their own existence not because they meet some measure of rationality or conform to a plan for how society ought to be organised, but because they represent a set of conventions or customs that have *proven* themselves to be productive of human flourishing and prosperity, and which have been passed on across generations as an inheritance. That they have proven themselves in such a way denotes that they contain some practical wisdom which might not necessarily otherwise be obvious.

Cultural Complacency

Our material affluence today compared to previous eras is obvious. But affluence has begotten hubris about how we got here. It is a hubris that has manifested itself in different ways. One version has gained greater currency in recent debate: the belief that the characteristics nourished by the bourgeois ethic are actually hardwired. In this view, self-sufficiency, industry and responsibility are 'timeless, natural qualities of the individual', rather than the hard-won product of a particular moral and social order. Will Hutton has recently articulated such a view with exemplary complacency. Humans, he writes,

> have an innate sense of proportionality of deserved rewards and punishment for whatever good or bad act they perform. Everyone alive has individual agency and can use it for better or for worse – the harder I work, the more I deserve to earn; equally, if I do something profoundly culpable, say, stealing from my trusted clients or being violent in private to my close family, the more I deserve greater punishment. This is a common understanding written into our DNA.[38]

A different iteration of this perspective holds that even if this system of moral values is a social rather than a naturally occurring phenomenon, it can still somewhat be taken for granted. This view is to be found in the work of many in the modern free market canon, and it represents a defective extension of that valid insight best expressed by the Scottish philosopher Adam Ferguson: that our rules and customs are certainly the 'result of human action, but not the execution of any human design'.[39] An erroneous deduction has been made from this principle that there is a 'givenness' to our moral framework, and that we must take it 'for granted', rather than proactively seeking to nurture it.[40]

From this perspective stems the often-repeated view that our chief political challenge is not how to preserve these cultural supports or maintain an economic system that promotes human flourishing, but how to generate economic growth that will in turn expand the 'means' to all our individual ends. Abundance and prosperity, it is argued, will minimise the salience of moral questions, reduce tensions over cultural and moral values, and render our spiritual and ethical inheritance superfluous. Our economic model will be able to unplug itself from its moral 'shell'; it will have no further need for its moral supports and can rest instead upon the perpetual growth of the economic 'machine'.[41] Perhaps eventually, with technological advancement, it will have no need of humans themselves.[42]

Conservatives historically played a vital role in protecting society from this hubris. They were the 'guardians of stability', responsible for the preservation of those moral values which supported our flourishing, and the institutions and conventions within which they found concrete expression. But in recent times, they have comprehensively failed to discharge this vital responsibility. Indeed, many have made common cause with those who would chip away at our cultural and moral inheritance in pursuit of some other political end.

Without these guardians standing watch, the moral foundations which sustain the free economy have been allowed to crumble. And they have crumbled largely because of the ascendency of an ideology that has acted like a social and cultural solvent: liberal rationalism.

Liberal Rationalism

Liberalism is not a single coherent philosophical edifice. It has taken on diverse forms across different temporal and geographical contexts. The liberalism of David Hume or Adam Smith that grew out of the empiricist tradition can be contrasted with the rationalist variant of Jeremy Bentham, the *Encyclopédistes*, or Jean-Jacques Rousseau.[43] And of course some aspects of the liberal mindset are in conformity with the fundamentals of personalism – particularly its respect for individuals as moral agents who are possessed of free will and entitled to make their own decisions.

But the version of liberalism that has come to predominate in the modern world has a greater specificity. In fact, it is a degeneration of the liberal mindset that thinkers have long warned might take place. And in its application, it is not merely *complacent* about the moral supports of our particular form of economic order, but positively hostile towards them. This version of liberalism we shall call *liberal rationalism*, and it is made up of two interactive strains of thought.

The first is what might be called 'liberationism', which is a particular account of human nature and human value. In the liberationist's eyes, humans are born perfectly free, but are then rendered subject to a myriad of society's constraints and restraints. This view holds that the liberation of the human being from these obligations is the highest end that can be sought.

This is effectively an inversion of the basic personalist principle – that morality can only take place in the sphere of individual decision-making, where a person is themselves confronted with the question of whether to choose right or wrong. Liberationism holds not that an individual must be free to do good, but that *to be free is to be good*; that freedom is not the condition of morality, but its *essence*.

Such a view of freedom has a number of implications. First of all, it encourages us to believe that freedom and responsibility are dissociable. Liberationism holds responsibility to be a constraint or a hindrance upon freedom – something from which the individual ought to be 'liberated'. Liberationism thus aims at the systematic decoupling of rights from duties. And this makes it deeply corrosive of the values of ownership too, for to own is to incur obligations – to communities, to a culture, to an inherited moral matrix. Liberationism aims instead at the enjoyment of freedom without attendant duties.

Liberationism does not deny the *existence* of obligations or responsibilities. But it contends that only those forms of obligation that are freely chosen are legitimate. Those incurred by virtue of being born into a particular family, country or even gender lack such a legitimacy, unless they are explicitly consented to – and even then they are to be treated sceptically. Here, political obligation arises from consent, not from one's membership of a community, be it the family, the nation, or indeed humankind itself. To that end, its theory of obligation is, as Yoram Hazony has put it, really 'a theory of the individual's freedom *from* political obligation'.[44]

This makes liberationism instinctively *presentist*: it is an ideology that extricates people from a temporal continuum that binds them to the past and the future. In breaking that continuum, liberationism, as Tocqueville put it, 'makes men forget their ancestors, but also hides their descendants and keeps them apart from their fellows. It constantly brings them back to themselves and threatens in the end to imprison them in the isolation of their own hearts.'[45]

Because liberationism rejects the idea that freedoms arise from constraint – that my right to something necessarily implies a duty on others to recognise that right – there is a pathological element to liberationism's conception of freedom: in seeking to emancipate people from those things which provide an inner restraint or discipline, it also diminishes the very sense of obligation to others that makes freedom possible. Without the inner restraint that responsibility imbues, the need for an overweening authority to restrain and govern our interactions with each other grows.[46]

There is a further pathological dimension to liberationism too. For if to be good is merely to be free, then the natural, human instinct towards the obligations of community becomes in some way irrational. And liberationism is thus led to seek some tool or instrument to free individuals from the social context from which they derive comfort and belonging – to 'force them to be free'.

The second salient aspect of this particular version of liberalism is its social rationalism. Social rationalism holds that the economic problem – that is, how scarce resources are to be allocated – can be reduced to a set of purely technical considerations. It is a 'positivist' style of thought that rejects the significance of all knowledge except that which can be verified by the senses. As such, it 'relentlessly ignores mankind as a spiritual or moral entity' and can only treat the moral and spiritual supports of socio-economic arrangements as 'irrationalities' that ought to be discarded.[47] In *Rationalism in Politics*, Michael Oakeshott offers a compelling description of the social rationalist:

> Much of his political activity consists in bringing the social, political, legal and institutional inheritance of his society before the tribunal of his intellect, and the rest is rational administration, reason exercising an uncontrolled jurisdiction over the circumstances of the case . . . The conduct of affairs, for the Rationalist, is a matter of solving problems . . . in this activity the character which the Rationalist claims for himself is the character of the engineer, whose mind (it is supposed) is controlled throughout by the appropriate technique.[48]

Social rationalism isn't to be confused with scientific reasoning *in general*. Instead, it denotes the concerted application of technical reasoning to socio-economic problems. In the case of the economy, the social rationalist contends that the cultural supports we've discussed *can* be replaced by purely technical reasoning, and *ought to* be, since technical reasoning is 'more efficient'. The economy does not appear to the social rationalist as part of a broader moral universe. Rather, it is like a machine – a 'self-dependent process whirring away automatically' – and it is best managed by those technical experts or engineers who have been instructed in how to operate it.[49]

Social rationalism and liberationism are thus effectively unified in common cause: to dislocate the economy from the moral and social conditions that would inevitably put constraints on its running. For the liberationist, this dislocation is necessary to render individuals more perfectly 'free'. For the social rationalist, it enables the technicians to exercise greater control over the economic machine. The great irony is that, rather than yielding a society of limited government and free, independent individuals, the liberationist and social rationalist currents within contemporary liberalism have instead strengthened the case for an expanded state as the instrument through which their ideals are to be realised.

If, as social rationalism maintains, economic questions are purely technical, then there is no moral component to the question of what level a certain decision should be taken at, or which entity or form of association should fulfil a given social function, and so on. Rather, these questions are simply a matter of aligning the means available with the ends sought in the most efficient manner possible. Since the state appears to the social rationalist as 'a vast reservoir of power', and since 'the most effective, certain and speedy way of reaching a given end will seem to be to direct all available resources' towards a particular goal, an inherent logic follows within social rationalism towards the augmentation of the state's functions and power.[50]

This expansion of the state's role in the economy and society holds out the possibility of securing the end of liberationism too. If liberationism teaches people to hate responsibility, a powerful state tempts them into believing that human desires and rights can indeed be provided for without the need for anyone to shoulder responsibility. The individual can simply be relieved of their responsibilities – to care for the elderly, to raise children, to make provision for the future – by outsourcing them to the state.

All of these trends depend on a totally revised conception of the economy – from one part of an integrated moral order to a sort of morally neutral, *self-standing* machine the purpose of which is not human flourishing, but the satisfaction of people's desires and their release from obligation.

For liberal rationalists, responsibility ceases to be 'reckoned' among people's rights as a vital complement to freedom, and instead becomes an encumbrance.[51] Providing for the vicissitudes of life is no longer a direct and personal commission of all capable people, but something that can be outsourced to the collective, or perhaps to some future generation who are unable to object to the burden they are expected to bear. Most radically, liberal rationalism transforms the idea of freedom from what Lord Action described as 'the right of being able to do what we ought' into 'the power of doing what we like' – a commitment to *liberty* as the counterpart of responsibility has been transmuted into a veneration of *license*.[52]

The idea of the economy as autonomous and self-standing eventually degenerates into the view that it is *self-serving* – that it has its own inner rationality and its own ends, to which society can be used as a means. More liberated individuals, freer labour markets, reduced responsibility for social provision – these are not methods for achieving some *thing*, they are 'the thing to be achieved'.[53] At this point, the place of the individual person disappears. The *amoral* economy becomes the *immoral* economy, a means to use and manipulate people.

This proneness of the liberal rationalist worldview towards an economic instrumentalism is not speculative. It can be seen, for instance, in the work of economist John Maynard Keynes, who in his own words 'recognised no moral obligation, no inner sanction, to control or obey', 'repudiated entirely customary morals, conventions and traditional wisdom', and considered himself 'in the strict sense of the term' an 'immoralist'.[54] Economics for him was a technical problem that should be confronted by government on the basis of rational expediency, not inherited moral values. It can be glimpsed, too, in the arguments of those such as Will Hutton, who assert that Britain must achieve a union of progressive 'liberalism' and 'socialism' which will 'liberate' us from 'the deadweight legacy' of culture and enrich us via 'Keynesian economics and planning'.[55] And it can be observed in the assumptions of those economists like Richard Murphy and Stephanie Kelton, who contend that moral concerns about debt, self-sufficiency and obligation are 'myths' which should not obstruct the government from using tax and spending to 'manage the economy' to achieve its 'desired outcomes'.[56] All these different approaches to the economy hold that culture itself, in the words of Torsten Bell, is a 'barrier to progress' – the progress of economic engineering.[57]

Liberal rationalism is essentially a steriliser, which empties society of the conditions that made human flourishing possible and leaves it grasping for some alternative source of security. It leads, paradoxically, to the situation which Tocqueville wrote of so clairvoyantly in the nineteenth century that it is worth quoting at length:

> I see an innumerable crowd of men, all alike and equal, turned in upon themselves in a restless search for those petty, vulgar pleasures with which they fill their souls. Each of them, living apart, is almost unaware of the destiny of all the rest . . . Above these men stands an immense and protective power which alone is responsible for looking after their enjoyments and watching over their destiny. It is absolute, meticulous, ordered, provident, and kindly disposed. It would be like a fatherlike authority, if, fatherlike, its aim were to prepare men for manhood, but it seeks only to keep them in perpetual childhood. It prefers its citizens to enjoy themselves, provided they only have enjoyment

> in mind. It works readily for their happiness but wishes to be the only provider and judge of it. It provides their security, anticipates and guarantees their needs, supplies their pleasures, directs their principal concerns, manages their industry, regulates their estates, divides their inheritance. Why can it not remove from them entirely the bother of thinking and the troubles of life?[58]

The Demoralisation of Mass Man

The consequences of all this for the human character have been acute. Liberal rationalism depersonalises the individual; its conception of men and women as desiring merely more absolute freedom is at odds with how humans really are: part individualistic but equally part social. It also causes the 'demoralisation' of people in the original sense of the word: it erodes their moral convictions. In seeking to divorce the rights of individuals from their responsibilities, it minimises people's opportunity for moral development. In fact, it fosters the idea that individuals can do without external moral props entirely – that they are innately self-sufficient. But by ejecting individuals from their social settings and alienating them from a moral inheritance that once provided surety and confidence, liberal rationalism ends up generating a mass of atomised, uncertain, insecure men and women who 'have been ground down . . . into mere particles of social dust'.[59] Liberal rationalism transforms unique *persons* of inherent dignity into *individuals* who are liable to be counted, interchanged and discarded.

All of this explains a further, sociological consequence of liberal rationalism, and one of paramount importance for the case advanced in this book: the diminution of personal ownership, which can be observed by trends in both the private economy and in the expansion of the state.

In the first case, ownership formerly provided the ethical basis for the free economy, such that it was legitimate in the eyes of those who participated in it. Self-interestedness and mere acquisitiveness could never play this role alone. The idea that economic freedoms came with corresponding duties and obligations – to those that one was transacting with, to the wider community in which economic activity took place – tempered the market and rendered it morally acceptable. But having thinned this sense of ownership in British society, liberal rationalism has allowed a business culture to emerge which holds that greed can somehow be good, or that 'private vices' might actually produce 'public benefits', as Bernard Mandeville once cynically put it. In such a culture, zero-sum interactions proliferate, and the legitimacy of the free economy is undermined.

Examples of this in our economy today are legion. Take, for example, the phenomenon of 'fleecehold', in which a developer sells the rights to manage the communal areas and roads of a housing estate to a private company. Freeholders who move into the new properties are left at the mercy of these companies, who can then arbitrarily charge whatever level of 'service fee' they like without any input or consent from residents. In the past, large landowners often used a leasehold model to retain a degree of control over the properties they owned. They did so because they considered themselves to have obligations both to their occupants – to maintain the properties in good condition – and to the wider community – to ensure the appearance of the properties enhanced the surrounding area rather than blemished it. That idea of responsibility now gone, we are left with housing developers who scar existing communities in order to extract cash from new residents. And while some new protections for leaseholders have been introduced via recent legislation, they do not go nearly far enough.

Or consider the financial services sector, which has long been a vital asset for our economy – centuries before even the 'Big Bang' reforms of the 1980s. Among other things, it provides the means by which we are able to make long-term investments in our country, so future generations might be more prosperous than our own. But some activity in the City has become highly short-termist. This is obviously true in the case of quantitative trading firms, which employ some of the very brightest minds in the world to shave fractions of milliseconds off arbitrage opportunities to make money without providing any wider social value. But it also applies to certain private equity business models too.

Macquarie Group's ownership of Thames Water has recently provided an emotive flashpoint, as billions were paid out in dividends between 2006 and 2017 even as its debt has ballooned to over £20 billion and its infrastructure continues to creak. In fact, Macquarie also owned Wightlink, a ferry company operating across the Solent to the Isle of Wight, and 'which under its control saw borrowing increase to pay shareholders, with corresponding timetable reductions, the near doubling of ticket prices and a lack of investment in ferry upgrades'.[60] Further examples of short-termism in the modern corporate world can be found in the activities of certain private companies towards the pension policies of the firms they acquire. HIG Capital bought Silentnight – a mattress manufacturer based in Yorkshire – and managed to cut staff pensions, while passing on the liabilities to the Pension Protection Fund, which is funded by taxpayers.[61]

None of this is inherent in the private equity business model. A vibrant economy depends on individuals and firms taking risks and bearing the financial consequences for that risk-taking. But absent a sense of responsibility and obligation, that risk-taking can be extractive and exploitative, rather than mutually beneficial. And as a result, the free economy appears increasingly casino-like to those subject to its vicissitudes, and therefore increasingly illegitimate. If the business world is unable to present itself as recognising wider obligations and higher ethical purposes, then the calls for government to direct, regulate and control will multiply.

Which brings us to the second area in which the decline of ownership is having a very material effect: the heightened prominence of the state in our lives. It is often presumed that the growth of the state has been driven by those who are ideologically committed to a larger role for government. And, granted, advocates of statism have always sought to expand the government when they've had the chance – often in conjunction with what Hilaire Belloc called those 'practical men' and women who think that all socio-economic problems are technical and best solved by a powerful state.[62]

But the truth is that the conditions for the growth of the state were not generated *ex nihilo* by advocates of statism. Those conditions – in particular the willingness of vast numbers of people to give up responsibility for the management of their lives to some overarching authority – were produced specifically by liberal rationalism and its demoralising, depersonalising effects on society. The 'mass man' produced by this demoralisation cannot help but be hostile to an economic system which has levered him out of his communities and made his existence so precarious. But nor can he help being entirely receptive to the promise that his security and well-being might be supplied by a benevolent state.[63] If the economy he participates in feels anarchic and brutish, who can blame him for wanting it to be more regulated, more directed, more managed?

British people have been deprived of that desire to have control and autonomy which used to be the 'lifegiving creative force' of our way of life.[64] In so many areas, we have given up obligations that were previously met at a personal or intimate level within families and communities. Care for elderly relatives used to be the preserve of family members. Now, we load that responsibility onto local governments. Instead of encouraging families to take responsibility for their retirement provision, the government does it for them. Rather than asking people to take ownership for their health and well-being, the government proposes to simply ban smoking over time, or levy higher taxes on unhealthy foods. Instead of families supervising their children to brush their teeth or to feed them before school, we ask the state to do it for us.

None of this is costless. The government has to absorb an ever-growing proportion of our annual revenue as a country to discharge those various responsibilities we have outsourced. But there is another price to be paid, too: as responsibility floats upwards to the state, the right to make decisions about how people ought to live and interact with each other follows closely behind. And where once the soft authority of a shared moral inheritance helped to order society, the hard power of the state in the form of legislation and regulation is now required to order our conduct. In this environment, the scope for humans to use their own initiative to address social problems narrows.

The culmination of this process belies the liberationist fantasy that rights and freedoms could ever be divorced from responsibilities. Liberal rationalism fashioned a people hostile towards the idea of being responsible for themselves and for those proximate to them and susceptible to the appeal of a strong state, which promised them security and safety, if they'd give up just a little more of their freedom. The social basis for the legitimacy of our free economy has been thoroughly deconstructed. Now, the state sits heavy atop our social structure, and in the absence of that web of obligations and the various forms of community that used to define social existence, it bears down on the atomised individuals beneath it, sinking further and further into their lives.

Hence we see that the growth of the state is not first and foremost an economic development, but a *cultural* one. It is the cumulative effect of a political ideology which is hostile to the things that formerly kept the state in check: a social structure and a moral framework dedicated to the principles of personal ownership. Likewise, the fact that our savings and investment rates are some of the lowest among advanced economies, productivity has flatlined for decades, and *growth* has languished is not due to some failure of economic technique. It is the upshot of an economy which has been emptied of its moral sustenance.

The Statist Imperative

Of course, there have always been a range of functions that the state has been required to discharge because it is the only institution capable of doing so. But the liberal rational paradigm envisages no in-built checks on the expansion of the state's remit. Quite the contrary – it creates an *imperative* for the state to solve all problems. It thus creates the conditions in which statism can thrive – and these are the conditions in which the human person is eventually transformed from a subject of inherent value into a mere means.

This applies most obviously to questions of social provision. If the questions of who ought to provide for the care of elderly relatives, or who is best placed to raise children, or who should be responsible for personal health are held to be merely matters of delivering efficient outcomes, then it *seems* rational for those responsibilities to be assumed by the state, for it is the site of maximum technical power in society. Liberal rationalism cares only for what is decided, and not *who* decides – it cannot conceive that there might be intrinsic rather than merely instrumental reasons for children or the elderly to be cared for by those close to them, or for local communities to be able to look after the needy in their area more directly.

But the material upshot of this line of thought is that the state must collect more and more in taxation to fund the provision of those services. And when it becomes apparent that the state is actually much less capable of discharging those functions than the individual or the proximate community, the conditioned response is not to question whether it is right for a growing suite of responsibilities to be outsourced to the state, or whether there might be important considerations to be made about how we all care for one another beyond mere efficiency. Rather, it is to suggest that the state needs more power, and more control over people's lives. And so the funding requirement for state services ratchets upwards.

More often than not, however, we deem it easier to fund the state's activities not through higher taxation on present generations, but by drawing on future ones. We do this by running budgetary deficits which we fund through borrowing. The public, stripped of the ethic of ownership, is only too willing to shift the burden onto future taxpayers.

The diminution of ownership is also driving the vast liabilities that are being generated in the provision of the state pension, which will demand escalating tax funding and thus have an increasingly suffocating effect on the economy. Instead of individuals making their own financial provisions for old age and retirement, the state has guaranteed – 'triple locked' – a level of pension provision that (especially in the context of demographic ageing) will involve ever-higher costs for the taxpayer. We currently spend about £140 billion on the state pension, or 5 per cent of GDP – more than we spend on education, and over twice as much as what we spend on defence. By the 2070s, it is estimated that it will cost about 8 per cent of GDP, or about 50 per cent more than today.[65]

The situation is more dire when it comes to those directly employed by the state, whose pensions entitlements alone represent a financial liability greater than the stated size of the national debt.[66] This 'ponzi scheme', in which contributions from future pensioners pay for the living costs of present ones, could only be possible in a society deprived of the conviction that to provide for oneself as far as possible is a moral duty.

Eventually, the liberal rationalist paradigm permits people to forget that the state provision of services is not an end in itself but exists simply to serve human needs. After that point, state services become the end to which human persons are but means. The more prosaic forms of this distortion can be found in attitudes to things like the state provision of childcare, whereby the importance of childcare is seen as secondary to the imperative of expanding the workforce, or in that inhumane approach to immigration which sees every new migrant simply as an extra head to boost total annual production. But it is to be found in more sinister forms too. Perhaps the most nightmarish is the argument by some commentators that we ought to consider the expansion of euthanasia services in order to ease pressure on the National Health Service. 'We cannot afford a taboo on assisted dying', writes Matthew Parris:

> It may sound brutal, but I don't apologise for . . . treat[ing] human beings as units – in deficit or surplus to the collective. For a society as much as for an individual, self-preservation must shine a harsh beam on to the balance between input and output. To protect its future, a healthy society must adapt its norms, its cultural taboos and its moral codes.[67]

In Parris's view, ending people's lives more swiftly will help to alleviate the fiscal pressures on a particular government department.

Old Dogmas

This statist imperative is also now frequently applied to the question of how we build a stronger economy. Within the liberal rationalist paradigm, variables like investment rates, labour productivity, or the propensity to consume or save are not the organic features of a particular people or society, but mechanical features of the economy that can be manipulated through the application of technique.

This strain of thinking is deeply embedded in British political and economic thought. Take the subject of investment. That a lack of investment is an acute problem for the British economy is uncontroversial. It is widely considered the key reason for our low productivity growth. But liberal rationalists see this fundamentally as a technical problem: to rectify it, they place their faith in what the present Labour government describes as a more powerful, 'active' state, which simply does the investing on our behalf, either by raising taxes for the purpose or directing credit towards its chosen objectives. All of this explains its recent efforts to change the way we measure government debt in Britain by netting it off against the totality of government assets. This was done not to give a more reliable picture of the public finances, but to 'free up' room for the government to borrow more. As Ben Zaranko put it, however, 'a technical change to debt definitions' does not change 'fiscal reality'; eventually, such borrowing will have to be paid for by the public.[68]

Mariana Mazzucato, an influential Italian-American economist, offers an archetypal liberal rationalist conception of how to solve the investment problem in her book *The Entrepreneurial State*. What is needed, she argues, is not a renewed focus on the people that make up our society – their motivations, their interests, their values – but a 'systems perspective', from which the 'visible hand' of the state can not only 'nudge' but 'push' society towards its own investment priorities. None of this is ideological in the liberal rationalist view: it is sound economic technique – the advocacy of 'policies that work', writes Mazzucato.[69]

As liberal rationalists think about how the state can more 'actively and courageously' save and invest on our behalf, little attention is paid to the moral or cultural dispositions that might promote real saving and investment in our society – on the one side, the values of thrift and the propensity to defer consumption, and on the other, the legitimacy of risk-taking and esteem for the entrepreneur. In fact, higher taxes and higher borrowing shrink both the capacity of individuals and businesses to invest and the potential benefits of doing so – and, in thus destroying private savings and investment, liberal rationalism makes us even more dependent on the state to do these things for us.

This attitude towards investment is a source of inflationary pressures, too. In the long term, if investment is not to be covered by current savings, it must either be funded through credit expansion, or through the importation of savings from abroad.

The consequence is either inflation, which itself reduces the incentives to save and thus intensifies the investment dilemma, or dependency on foreign capital, which creates its own problems for the sustainability of the economy.

All of this crystallises another deleterious effect of the liberal rationalist approach, which is that in its desire to manipulate the economy, it demands further state intervention. 'Securonomics' – one version of contemporary liberal rationalist thinking popular on the British left – contends that the state ought to guarantee workers some level of economic security, which they propose to provide via increases to the statutory minimum wage and by tightening the regulations around employment rights. These measures are supposed to deliver improvements to labour productivity, and therefore increase economic growth.

The reality, however, is that none of this deals with the real sources of low productivity, such as impaired incentives for industry and enterprise, or to invest in capital and training. And in practice, the additional requirements placed upon businesses by securonomics will have all sorts of adverse outcomes – from inflation (as remuneration becomes disconnected from output) to a shrinking job market (as employers find that taking on additional workers is financially unviable), or to more people leaving the workplace because the demands of low-wage employment have intensified as businesses seek higher output to offset their increased costs. Regardless, the result will be a greater number of people dependent on the state for support, fewer people paying taxes to fund that support, and consequently even more pressure to borrow.

Arguably, the culmination of liberal rationalist thinking today is to be found in the emergent body of thought called Modern Monetary Theory. It embraces the idea that governments like that of the United Kingdom which issue their own currency are liberated from constraints about public expenditure; such governments will always be able to meet spending commitments because they 'can never run out of money', as one prominent theorist puts it. Debt, its advocates contend, is thus never a problem for currency issuers. Through the Modern Monetary Theory lens, the state is at the centre of the economic 'universe', not the taxpayer or the household, nor even the business. In its upside-down world, taxes are not for funding public services (for which government can simply print more money), but for micromanaging the economy. In fact, taxation is really about the government 'provisioning' itself; 'it's there to get people working and producing things for the government'.[70] These are no longer fringe views; they have found a receptive audience on the British left, and a keen political advocate in the form of Zack Polanski, the leader of the Green Party.[71]

These various contemporary advocates of liberal rationalism present their ideas as novel, developmentalist approaches to the economy. But they are simply the latest iterations of a very old, statist dogma: one that considers increasing the productive output of the economy to be a scientific task best prosecuted by a centralised power; that supposes the state and its technicians know better how to invest than individuals and businesses; and which promises a greater degree of economic security if only people would concede more choice in their lives.

Nevertheless, we should be more concerned by the fact that these ideas continue to catch on – by the fact that people in our country remain receptive to them. Statist worldviews regarding social provision and economic growth have gained ascendancy because we have collectively lost the intuitions about the economy and its place in a broader moral order that once provided a check on the size and scope of the state.

Philosophical Cul-de-sacs and the Conservative Alternative

It is soothing to think that all these damaging economic trends are the consequence of social-democratic policies implemented by governments of the left. But statist economics represents a response, however perverted, to problems generated by liberal rationalism – a mindset that is just as frequently held by governments of the *right*.

Perhaps it is understandable that we don't typically associate statism with the right. At every election, the Conservative Party states its intention to reduce the influence of the state in people's lives and to return power back to individuals. It is the Labour Party that invokes the state as the solution to more or less each and every potential public policy challenge. But the good intentions of conservatives are not enough. And Conservative Party policies over the last several decades have often promoted statism in practice, even if unintentionally.

When did the Conservative Party start accommodating liberal rationalism? When did it start paying less attention to those cultural foundations of our society which it traditionally considered itself duty bound to protect and maintain? Establishing precise timelines for deep cultural changes is difficult. It is true that an explicit alliance between Conservatism and liberalism was built from the 1970s onwards. Liberal ideas provided a direct counter to the Keynesian social democratic nostrums which had held the British economy in a stranglehold since the middle of the twentieth century and facilitated the one-way growth of government. Margaret Thatcher and her ministers drew directly and openly from Friedman, Hayek and Mises to make the case for social and economic liberty, often at the exclusion of the other values that go into promoting human flourishing. Keith Joseph, the pre-eminent intellectual force behind Thatcherism, was an admirer of Martin Weiner's book *English Culture and the Decline of the Industrial Spirit*, which argued that the nation's culture – its Christian traditions, its love of place, its respect for architectural traditions, even its bourgeois values – was an impediment to economic 'progress'.[72] He distributed a copy to every member of Thatcher's cabinet.

Yet Thatcher herself cannot reasonably be described as a liberal rationalist. She spoke explicitly of the free society having a 'moral basis' or a 'moral foundation', which she felt was located in 'the Judaeo-Christian outlook'. She pointed to how 'history has taught us that freedom cannot long survive unless it is based on moral foundations'. Elsewhere, she lamented that so much of contemporary economics has 'become more and more mathematical, and . . . less and less human'.[73]

She also affirmed the importance of moral responsibility – that 'we simply can't delegate the exercise of mercy and generosity to others'. And it is in this context that her most misunderstood quotation, that 'there is no such thing as society', should be understood. Thatcher recognised and valued society, if by that we mean 'the living tapestry of men and women' coexisting together. But she desperately wanted to avoid the tendency to pass on responsibility for socio-economic ills to the impersonal society or the abstract state. In that, she was an opponent of those cultural developments we have been tracing.[74]

Some of the unintended consequences of her policies have undoubtedly aided the liberal rationalist agenda, though. Deindustrialisation was instigated without a sense of what would continue to bind industrial communities together. Millions of homes were transferred from state ownership to private ownership, but not enough new homes were delivered, particularly in cities. The growth of the financial services sector was not accompanied by any serious thought about how we continue to attract capital to the parts of the economy that need it. And during her time in government, Thatcher failed to reform some of the most significant liberal rationalist institutions in Britain, such as the planning system or the health service, though these are more sins of omission, rather than commission.

It is probably truer, therefore, to say that Thatcher*ism* rather than Thatcher assisted the rise of the liberal rationalism that is doing such untold damage to British society. Indeed, part of the problem ever since has been that Conservative governments have pursued Thatcherite economics while forgetting about – and in so doing badly damaging – those external supports of the free economy, most inexplicably through mass immigration, multiculturalism and the continuous expansion of welfarism. It is this paradigm that must now be explicitly rejected.

Only a return to personalism can produce the type of thinking now required to retrieve the situation. A conservatism is needed which grasps that liberalism and statism are bound in a symbiotic relationship which is corrosive of our society's foundations. It must be consciously oriented towards expanding the scope for individual moral agency *and* rebuilding the communities in which this flourishing is possible; an approach which recognises '*all* aspects in which the human sense of self, on which human contentment and happiness in fact, depend'.[75] Only by doing these things simultaneously will we avoid compounding the individual-statist dialectic that has eroded the moral and social prerequisites of our economy, and in so doing led to this country's faltering economic performance.

The central theme running through the rest of this book is that the keystone of any programme to restore our economy must be the deliberate effort to diffuse ownership throughout our country. This entails not merely the wider ownership of tangible assets – although this is undoubtedly vital – but the *values* of ownership: ownership in that broad, moral sense of the term. Promoting ownership is how we unify freedom and responsibility into a mutually sustaining relationship once again. It is how we avoid the destructive dynamic that exists between these principles within liberal rationalism. And it is how we return the centre of gravity of social life back to the personal and the local, and how we renew the opportunities for people to flourish again.

But if the ends we seek are greater personal initiative and social responsibility, we must also reduce the instances in which the state is currently the principal agent and decision maker but ought not to be. To determine what those instances are, we first need a theory of what the state *should* be for.

2

What Is the State For?

[I]t is not just that statecraft should be soulcraft . . . statecraft is soulcraft. It is by its very nature. Statecraft need not be conscious of itself as soulcraft; it need not affect the citizens' inner lives skilfully, or creatively, or decently. But the one thing it cannot be, over time, is irrelevant to those inner lives.[1] – George Will

The modern history of Europe is littered with the projects of the politics of Rationalism. The most sublime of these is, perhaps, that of Robert Owen for 'a world convention to emancipate the human race from ignorance, poverty, division, sin and misery' . . . But not less characteristic are the diligent search of the present generation for an innocuous power which may safely be made so great as to be able to control all other powers in the human world, and the common disposition to believe that political machinery can take the place of moral and political education.[2] – Michael Oakeshott

The Rise of the State

Throughout British public discourse today, there is a fatalism about the role of the state in society. The move to a larger state is likely to be 'permanent', Paul Johnson of the Institute for Fiscal Studies has written.[3] Many believe that the complexity of modern life, the demands of demographic change or the increasing interconnectedness of the economy necessitates a bigger, more interventionist state to provide security and stability. 'Only government', it has been written by one popular economist, 'has the capacity to steer the transformation on the scale needed'.[4]

Former Prime Minister Tony Blair argues in his recent book *On Leadership* that debates around the size of the state or the role of individuals and communities 'have abated in significance even as they have intensified in fury', and that we ought to 'discard the ideology in favour of . . . the answer' – 'the *practical* answer'.[5] Such a fatalistic approach to the size of the state is a classic tenet of liberal rationalism – the view that as society gets more complex, only an ever-more powerful state will be up to the challenge of ordering it.

But the debates that Blair raises concerning the size of the state only feel old because they *are* old. In fact, they are perennial, and concern some of the most vital moral and political questions that any society must confront. And for those of us committed to personalism, given the world in which we find ourselves today, it's quite right – in fact, it's essential – that these debates remain of central importance. Arguments about the proper scope for state action could only have 'abated in significance' for those who are satisfied with the status quo.

The liberal rationalist worldview permits the notion that the state is omnicompetent – that it is potentially responsible for everything and anything – because it has no a priori argument for why certain problems should be solved by certain entities. It has no conception of 'subsidiarity' – of the idea that decision-making responsibility should rest at the most proximate level possible, and that the state should not deprive associations and communities of functions they can exercise themselves, but offer support and encouragement for such associations, and focus on competencies that only it can discharge.[6]

Seen simply as a vast concentration of power, the state holds out the possibility of solving a theoretically unlimited range of socio-economic problems, including how to generate growth itself. In this paradigm, it does not really make sense to ask what the state is for and not for – the answer to such a question is a simple function of whether it is the most efficient device for solving a problem. And so, liberal rationalism offers no in-built check upon the state's size and activities. Since it is more powerful than any one individual or any particular association of people, decision-making authority is inevitably dragged upwards away from the proximate and personal and towards the impersonal state. As Mariana Mazzucato tellingly puts it, '[t]he wrong question is: how much money is there and what can we do with it? The right question is: what needs doing and how can we structure [government] budgets to meet those goals?'[7]

Mazzucato's interest in the Apollo Programme as a model for economic development betrays the liberal rationalist conception of growth. In her book *Mission Economy*, she writes that what appeals to her about the space programme was that 'government had to break out of the conventions limiting its activities' to achieve the technical challenge of putting a man on the moon. It required considerable central direction and command and control, the sort of societal shift required in a wartime economy. 'If we can do it in wartime', she asks rhetorically, 'why not in peacetime, when the urgency is to solve societal battles and achieve common goals?'[8] The response, of course, is that economic growth is not a technical problem like space travel, but a symptom of broader societal health – that is, a function of complex organic processes that cannot be understood simply in terms of technique.

Some people also believe that by taxing people more and permitting greater state intervention, we are somehow acting more *morally*. In the past, these people tended to be on the far left – 'hot' socialists who believed in expansive public ownership and planning. Today, this tendency is more likely to appear in the form of the 'cool' statism of social democrats, who may not be wedded to state ownership but remain committed to the idea that, in Paul Collier's words, government is a 'morally superior vanguard' which knows best how to deliver maximally efficient outcomes for individuals.[9] It also appears in the arguments of provocateurs like the millionaire Gary Stevenson, who, rather than finding ways to use his own considerable means to improve the lives of those around him, instead demands that more of his – and other households' – income is taken by the state in the form of tax. What unites these various views is the idea that people ought not to be trusted with free choice and responsibility, and that it is preferable the state chooses for us.

This perspective even occasionally has some ostensibly conservative adherents too. Often, they appeal to the Burkean notion of the state as a partnership between the generations, or to the Conservatives who defended the social fabric from the predations of liberals in the nineteenth century and introduced significant social legislation on employee rights, housing and sanitation.[10] In particular, from this vantage point, the welfare state is an embodiment of the social solidarity that conservatives wish to preserve:

> Only Liberal ideologues, not Conservatives, see something fundamentally wrong with the welfare state as such. State provision for welfare is fully in accordance with Conservative principles. The welfare state is a thoroughly Conservative institution, which is why Conservatives did so much to bring it into existence.[11]

In the 'conservative' iteration of this idea, an active role for the state in social provision is acceptable if it expresses the majority views of the public, or if it fulfils the communitarian role of binding people together. Either way, by believing that the state can act as a moral agent on our behalf, we entertain the soothing notion that, as the role of government expands, our society somehow becomes more just and ethical.

We see the practical implications of this mode of thought everywhere. The state now penetrates more widely and more deeply into the lives of individuals and families. It provides for the raising of our children. It pays us a living when we are out of work. It takes complete responsibility for our health from cradle to grave. As these myriad activities expand, so too does the burden upon the economy for funding them. In 2024, Britain's GDP was £2.56 trillion; government spending that year added up to around £1.2 trillion. Between 1995 and the present, we have gone from a situation in which government spending consumes about a third of the economy, to one where it consumes about a half. And in roughly the same period, the number of people employed in the public sector or public sector–dominated industries has grown from 6.5 million to 10.7m – roughly a third of the entire workforce.

Moral Outsourcing

Of course, we have strong evidence that *even if* all our socio-economic questions were technical in nature, the state is rarely the most effective means of addressing them. We see this with economic growth, where well-intentioned interventions by the government to boost investment, for example, simply raise the cost of capital for the wealth-creating sector of the economy. But it is apparent in the delivery of social services too, where the cold, impersonal state is less effective at delivering care and support, for example, than close family or proximate community members.

And as the state has grown, it has also – and not coincidentally – become worse at the tasks that only it can perform. For one, our criminal justice system is inoperable: shoplifting is up by half since 2015; criminals are being let out of prison early not because they have been rehabilitated, but because there is insufficient prison capacity; tens of thousands of crown court cases are currently outstanding.[12] The state lacks any meaningful control over who enters and leaves this country – it finds it almost impossible to deport illegal criminals who are committing serious crimes on British streets. And the sustained neglect of our defence and security capabilities is becoming acutely clear. The size of the armed forces has shrunk by around two-thirds since the end of the Cold War. Defence expenditure as a proportion of the economy has roughly halved. The Royal Navy has fewer than twenty frigates or destroyers, of which only a proportion can currently be deployed. The state is increasingly both 'overfed and undernourished'.[13] The provision of order is the most essential function that the state is charged with. In Britain, it is failing conspicuously in this function, and this is undermining its very legitimacy.

Nevertheless, the principal argument against the view of the state as omnicompetent is not truly about efficiency. Rather, it is about the nature of a good society. For the liberal rationalist, we can all become better people simply by expanding the number of things that the state does for other people. For the personalist, however, a society in which the state substitutes for all of us as moral actors can only be defective, because it shrinks the space for personal initiative.

An illustration of this vital truth is to be found in the work of Hugh Cecil, an early twentieth-century Conservative parliamentarian and mentor to a young Winston Churchill. Imagine for a moment, he wrote in 1912, the example of the Good Samaritan:

> Suppose that instead of relieving the distressed man at his own cost, he had run after the priest and the Levite and by compulsion constrained them to come back and minister with their oil and their wine to the sufferings of the afflicted. Suppose he had required them to set the poor man upon their beast of burden and to take him to the inn, and had finally forced from each of them one or two pence which were necessary to pay the cost of entertainment. Does anyone suppose that the Good Samaritan

> would, after such acts, have been held up as the type of love of a Christian to his neighbour?[14]

Cecil's example is scriptural, but its relevance is universal. It would be ridiculous to go around earnestly thanking fellow taxpayers for their generosity in feeding the poor or caring for the sick through their taxes. The sort of goodness which permits personal moral development – the very purpose of a good society – consists in freely chosen acts and personal relationships; impersonal decisions made in the context of compulsion unavoidably have a diminished effect upon moral character.

That does not mean that collective actions can never have a moral dimension. Our nation's decision to resist the Nazis in the Second World War, for example, was irrefutably *good* – a collective moral endeavour that was nevertheless facilitated by state coercion. Equally, a social safety net which protects people from destitution ought reasonably to be seen as the collective expression of social solidarity for the poor and needy, even if it involves little *choice* on the part of contributors. And finally, the state has a role in transmitting those inherited values which constitute the basic operating system of our society, and which furnish people with the conditions to live good lives.

But there is a point beyond which the state's activities begin to take place at the expense of our ability to flourish, and that is when it *substitutes* for individuals and communities rather than supporting them, replacing voluntary acts of generosity or altruism with compulsion. At such a moment, people cease to consider their personal obligations to others, and look to the state to meet these obligations instead. We come to speak of rights and entitlements without recognising that these always imply corresponding responsibilities upon others – responsibilities which if they are not recognised voluntarily must be imposed compulsorily.

A decent society is one that affords as much space as possible for people to freely give their time, their energy and their resources to others, for it is in such free choices that humans transcend their condition and flourish as moral beings. And it is not in giving oneself to abstract ideas that this moral development takes place, but in doing so to real persons.[15] State support for the neediest is undoubtedly a collective good. But it does not have the same effect on an individual as the free and human act of giving to another. As the state plays an ever-expanding role in our lives, so we are all deprived of such opportunities for flourishing.

We learn a natural sense of obligation to others in the contexts of family and community, in which life is defined by real and proximate relationships between persons. The state cannot substitute for those forms of association, not least because it is based upon more abstract relations between people, but also because, as we have seen, the state's relationship with the forms of association that sit between it and individuals is fundamentally parasitical. It was not a 'direct outgrowth of family, tribe, or local community', but rather developed 'in circumstances of powerful opposition to kinship and other traditional authorities'.[16] In the liberal rationalist paradigm, the state has helped to liberate the individual primarily by degrading these communities; for statists, these same communities are a hindrance to the ability of the government to control the actions of individuals and must therefore be eliminated.

Ultimately, an expanding state reflects less an increased sense of charitableness or generosity among the public, and more an increasing willingness to outsource responsibility for confronting our shared social challenges – a willingness burnished by those who argue that socio-economic problems are entirely technical, and that having the state address them on our behalf will not only lead to more efficient solutions but also free us all to get on with our own individual concerns.

In part, a bigger state also indicates our changing attitudes towards risk. Risk is inherent to the human condition: it is by taking on risk that we innovate, learn, grow and discover. We also must take risks to do good – to try an untested method of meeting a need, or to put ourselves at the service of others without total foresight of what that might require. A well-adjusted society is one in which individuals are able to weigh up risks, make decisions and be accountable to those around them for the outcomes of their actions. Increasingly, however, we demand that the state assume this responsibility and insulate us from risk through legislation and regulation.

This has two problems. First, risks are never single: by eliminating one risk, we invariably create others. By trying to eliminate all risks in the course of farming and food production, for example, we increase the risk that farming will cease to be profitable in this country, that farmers will sell up, and that the beautiful English landscapes which we enjoy because of the stewardship of those who work the land will be lost forever. By trying to totally eliminate all risks to bats in each area of potential new residential development, we increase the risk that a chronic shortage of housing prevents young people from becoming property owners.

Second, the attempt to insulate ourselves from risk entirely deprives us of something essential to our moral development. 'Rational beings', Roger Scruton puts it,

> can flourish only when they have risks to confront and responsibility to assume. The risk-free life is not a life in which we are or can be fulfilled. Any pattern of thought that seeks to extinguish risk and to lift our responsibility in the face of it is, therefore, one that threatens a primary human need.[17]

Risk is never eliminated through state regulation – it is simply shifted around. In fact, what regulation really involves is the transfer of *responsibility* for judging between risks from individuals, families and communities to the state. But to effect that transfer is also to deprive people of the decision-making responsibility that enables them to live morally.

The Myth of the Nightwatchman State

The state is not and cannot be for everything. But it is not for nothing either. Conservatives desire not the absence of government, but to be quietly and effectively governed. Indeed, those in favour of a *smaller* state have often fundamentally undermined their case by reducing the state's ability to do those things which are obviously and unavoidably within its remit. This is perhaps one of the worst legacies of the Conservative coalition years, which simply introduced blanket reductions across the entirety of its activities rather than taking a genuine view about what the state ought and ought not to do.

At the same time, liberals have committed a categorical error in assuming that the advocacy of a small state is tantamount to the advocacy of a *neutral* state. It's a position largely drawn from the harm principle advanced by John Stuart Mill, which contends that interference with people's liberty is never justified except if it is to protect others, and that trying to influence people's conduct through authority is inherently wrong. It is usually invoked by those who imagine that our social, economic and political institutions can subsist without an underpinning moral framework.

Of course, what is not at stake is the idea that the state ought to be neutral or 'blind' when it comes to the application of the law, for example, or in how it adjudicates between domestic market competitors. But the broader liberal notion of the 'watchman' state has a deeply self-destructive logic which we can see playing out in real time in Britain. For no society can afford to be neutral when it comes to the values that are essential to the maintenance of a particular way of life. Liberal rationalism's assumption that the things it holds dear – especially freedom – are self-standing and self-sufficient has infected much policymaking in Britain and has gravely inhibited the state's ability to police the borders – both literal and metaphorical – of our free society.

While the state cannot flourish on our behalf, it has a vital duty in furnishing those conditions which will enable people to flourish. The idea of a neutral state is built on a sort of social version of the efficient market hypothesis. This 'efficient society hypothesis' contends that the state need not proactively support the thing that will enable people to develop as personalities; that is, it contends that family life, or values around enterprise and personal responsibility, or the presence of cohesive local communities, are optional extras, rather than the vital supports of our peculiar form of society. Yet in neglecting these things, the idea of the neutral state creates the conditions that undermine the free society: in the absence of the soft power of shared values, customs and conventions, the hard power of the state is required to ensure order.

But it is not simply the case that the state ought to have a bearing on these matters. It is that it inescapably *does*. As George Will put it, 'it is not just that statecraft should be soulcraft . . . statecraft *is* soulcraft. It is by its very nature.'[18] It might be soothing for liberals to think that the neutrality they advocate keeps them out of the debate between conflicting cultures and therefore plays some pacific function. But the truth is that neutrality is in fact its *own* cultural position – a sort of anti-culture, which ends up favouring the atomised, the depersonalised and the demoralised at the expense of the cohesive, the solid and the durable.

The Cincinnatus State

At the political level, the inability of the right to offer a coherent philosophy of what the state is and is not for – a consequence of the liberal conservative tendency to claim that the state has *no* role at all – has put it at a continual disadvantage in relation to those who believe fervently in the state having an expansive, determinative role in our lives. For whereas social democrats are committed to some idea of what the state should do, conservatives have generally only been interested in ensuring that whatever the state does is fiscally sustainable.

The result is that conservatives are always worrying about the total *size* of the government budget rather than its *shape*, and as a consequence are 'always trying to bring leftist budgets into balance'.[19] Statists have thus set the direction of government activity, while the right has simply helped to determine how fast our society moves in that direction.

But the true conservative vision of the state is not simply a leaner, more frugal version of the social rationalist approach. It is not simply 'fiscally sustainable statism'. It is a distinctive, morally inflected view of the state's proper sphere of activities that is based upon personalism – upon the belief in the dignity of humans as moral agents who find their sense of identity and meaning not from their cold relationship with the state, but from genuine community. And it is now increasingly urgent that this view is set out.

For years, the core of that conservative view has been the position expressed pithily by Adam Smith in the mid-eighteenth century – that 'little else is requisite to carry a state to the highest degree of opulence from the lowest barbarism, but peace, easy taxes, and a tolerable administration of justice'.[20] The state's three central functions were, Smith wrote in *The Wealth of Nations*,

> the duty of protecting the society from violence and invasion of other independent societies . . . the duty of protecting, as far as possible, every member of society from the injustice of oppression of every other member of it, or the duty of establishing an exact administration of justice; and thirdly, the duty of erecting and maintaining certain public works, and certain public institutions, which it can never be for the interest of any individual, or small number of individuals, to erect and maintain.[21]

This was part of the system of what he called 'natural liberty', in which the state's activities never ought to be considered ends in themselves, but rather means towards enhancing the ability of free people to act, interact and cooperate spontaneously.

It is largely this same vision of the role of the state that Hayek articulated in the twentieth century. Hayek's argument for the rule of law was underpinned by the contention that if the individual is to remain the key decision-making agent in society, the state ought to create rules that apply generally: the state ought to create a framework in which people could make their own decisions, rather than issue directives through which the state would make decisions on our behalf:

> The state should confine itself to establishing rules applying to general types of situation, and should allow the individuals freedom in everything which depends on the circumstances of times and place, because only the individuals concerned in each instance can fully know these circumstances and adapt their actions to them . . . the more the state 'plans', the more difficult planning becomes for the individual.[22]

This is the difference, Hayek argued, between 'the rule of law' and 'planning'; 'between providing signposts and commanding people which road to take'.[23]

Defence, policing, a stable monetary system and border policy, the maintenance of road networks and public transportation: all these things constitute important parts of Hayek's conception, as with Smith's, of the state's proper role. They are 'instrumental' functions: tasks that individuals and smaller communities cannot discharge themselves, but that are essential for people to go about their lives. This framework also recognises the necessity of a minimum level of sustenance for those not able to support themselves – a level that ought to gradually rise as society itself grows more affluent.

This remains a sturdy basis upon which a conservative theory of the state ought to be built. It has an Oakeshottian principle at its heart: that the state ought not to be omnicompetent – stretching its power and influence into the 'minuteness' of social existence – it should instead be 'paramount' within a 'narrow' set of activities.[24] Today, this theory demands not haircutting government spending across the full range of the state's competencies, but deliberately reducing spending on some of them in order to invest better in other ones.

Alone, however, this understanding of the state is not sufficient for the task. Reducing the size of the state is only worthwhile if it helps to replenish those vital sources of human endeavour, and therefore our collective prosperity. Hayek, by his own admission, was not a conservative, but a liberal, and was thus content to take those moral and cultural supports for granted – to 'presume' them, as he said himself.[25]

But it is no longer enough to take these things for granted. Today, simply extricating the state from certain areas of life will end up exaggerating the lack of robustness and self-sufficiency which we have identified, ironically, as the foremost driver of demand for the state's growth. This is effectively the same dilemma discussed in the previous chapter; that in seeking to augment freedom in isolation, we may accelerate the processes of depersonalisation and demoralisation that have so harmed the vitality and initiative of our people. We have to reduce the high level of demand that currently exists for the state, in order to durably reduce its supply. And this means rebuilding the *social* contexts that enable people to live self-sufficiently. If we do this, the question of the size of the state should be able to answer itself.

'The most important human task is transmission' – the transmission from one generation to the next of those conditions that promote human flourishing, which have been established not through pure reason but learned through experience. The state has a vital role to play in the transmissions of those conditions, and in the political order that can sustain them. For those qualities cannot be presumed: they must be 'willed' – at least today, when presumption alone has been shown to be totally insufficient. 'The presuppositions of our polity must be supplied, politically.'[26]

The most important of these conditions is a shared moral framework anchored by the values of personal ownership. What we need is a 'Cincinnatus state': a state that, like the legendary statesman who saved the Roman Republic and then relinquished power, creates circumstances in which it no longer needs to be predominant. In other words, we require a programme for state-sponsored personalism and the reduction of dependency. This is something of a paradox in that it requires us to *use* the state to diminish its prominence in social and economic life. But we can understand this as 'prophylactic doses of government', akin to an inoculation.[27] Invigorating certain qualities in individuals and supporting certain forms of association that those individuals might benefit from will reduce the demand for the state's work and renew the contexts for flourishing. This, then, must be the basic rationale of a conservative theory of the state today: a state that is assertive in returning obligations to the level of the personal and the proximate.

The Responsible Society

If individuals and communities are going to assume responsibility for areas of social provision currently administered by the state, the cultural and sociological infrastructure that would make this possible needs to be rebuilt.

There have been abortive attempts at this rehabilitation before. Most recently, there was the Coalition Government's 'Big Society' programme, inspired in particular by Phillip Blond, a 'Red Tory' political philosopher. In the words of David Cameron, this was a programme to forge a 'stronger society' and 'a culture of responsibility in our country'. It was not some 'fluffy add-on' or 'optional extra': it was intended to be 'the key to transforming our economy, our society, our country's future'.[28]

In practice, however, this agenda *was* always treated as an optional extra. The Big Society failed to achieve its stated aims because it did not meaningfully transfer *social functions* away from the state to civil society. Those forms of community and association that have withered as the state has grown have done so because they have become increasingly function-*less*. Unfortunately, the Big Society programme did nothing to address this.

Take the charitable sector. Support for charities was meant to be a key component of the Big Society. On the face of it, this seemed promising: if there is to be a genuine repatriation of responsibility downwards, voluntary organisations will have to take on social functions currently undertaken by the state, from delivering social care and community transport, for example, to determining how land ought to be used. But although the charitable sector has grown since 2010, it has done so not as an *alternative* to state provision, but often as the state's *instrument*. A vast proportion of charitable funding now comes *from government* – instead of giving people choice about what causes or organisations they wish to support financially, the government taxes them and then directs that capital towards charitable organisations of its own choosing.

At the same time, numerous charities have become politicised entities, whose operating and staff costs exceed the amount of money going towards the causes they were set up to advance. This 'charity industrial complex', as it has been described by Guy Dampier, disburses money to organisations campaigning for reparations to the Global South, for the 'dismantling of white privilege', and for various other causes contrary to British interests, and contrary to what the public actually wants.[29] The voluntary sector is not, currently, a site of experimentation, in which associations of people offer ways to reduce the demand for state services. It is an expensive, state-subsidised advocacy industry.

To genuinely devolve power downwards, a government's overriding purpose must be to give individuals, associations and communities the opportunity to discharge real, everyday social functions that matter to people – like care provision for the young and old, or decision-making over how land is used, or responsibility for how savings are used or invested. For social rationalists, this is almost impossible to entertain, since it seems so contrary to the determined path towards greater centralisation that informs their worldview. But such a diffusion of power is not only possible; it is *essential* if we are to rebalance society in a way conducive to flourishing and prosperity.

The government ought not to think that this revitalised role for the community will necessarily take place in the same forms of old. Our failing over recent decades has just as much been a failure to 'create new contexts of association and moral cohesion' as it has been to restore long-standing ones.[30] It will be important for the state to support the development of new modes of social provision in both the market and voluntary sector as we transform the current, socialised system. But we also ought not rule out the possibility that those older forms of association, which have had their social functions wrested from them by the welfare state, might be repurposed and renewed.

Policy proposals to these ends will be explored in greater detail in a later chapter. But remaining at the level of principle for a moment, here are five major considerations for would-be reformers.

First, how do we go about empowering the most ancient form of association – the family? It has proven itself to be the best setting for raising children, caring for the elderly and for nurturing the sense that all generations have obligations to one another. It is the most essential and natural form of social support, a school of moral sentiments, and a vital medium for the transmission of culture. A smaller state demands stronger families. How do we go about fostering them?

Second, how can responsibility for deciding how land is used be pushed downwards? How might local communities get a genuine stake in determining their futures, such that their role in the planning system is transformed from the negative one of raising objections, to the positive one of shaping change?

Third, by what fiscal and financial mechanisms could voluntary or community organisations and associations become a genuine alternative to the state provision of services? People would be unlikely to fund the voluntary delivery of services if they are also compelled to fund those operated by the state. What would be the process by which people could choose to take responsibility back from the state again?

Fourth, how can the Cincinnatus state, as I have called it, proactively encourage this wider repatriation of responsibility? If, as I have argued, people's desire to take ownership of their lives has been damaged, what can be done to repair it? It is also certainly true that more well-off communities in our country, with more 'social capital', will be in a much better position to take ownership than others with less. How could ownership be promoted in less affluent places, such that personal responsibility does not become the preserve of the affluent?

Finally, what is the positive role for government within this proposed order? What are the functions that we will continue to demand that the state fulfil, and for which our governors need to take vastly more responsibility? How can we move from an omnicompetent and totally ineffectual government to a limited and highly effective one?

Underlying all of this will be another profound dilemma. By giving back to people the responsibility for meeting the challenges of social existence, we will give them the freedom to experiment and potentially build better services and stronger communities. But this also necessarily means giving them the freedom to fail in this endeavour. What level of risk are we collectively willing to permit in the pursuit of a society in which individuals, families and communities have real control over their lives again?

Statecraft as Soulcraft

The purpose of the state is not to be moral on our behalf; it is to 'cultivate the conditions' for morality – conditions in which individuals have the opportunity to be both free and responsible.[31] These conditions have been left to wither as a consequence of liberal rationalism. The mission of conservatism now is to find ways to restore them, and to ensure that the state can properly fulfil the functions it exists to provide: that is, to provide security from within and without, and to provide the legal and cultural framework for human flourishing.

Most conservatives agree that the state ought to be smaller. But what has been missing from the debate has been a proper consideration of who or what will replace the state in meeting those very real demands for support and assistance. Simply stripping back the state's activities without thought to what comes next is inadequate when the moral resources that previously would have enabled people to be self-sufficient have been entirely exhausted. Conservatism, if it is to succeed, must focus on replenishing those resources. That starts with returning social functions to families and voluntary associations.

Reducing the size of the state appears to be a Sisyphean task, as the state continues to grow both in breadth and depth of activity. There are so many people with a vested interest in the expansion of state services – not least the majority who are now net beneficiaries of it, rather than contributors. But the state itself is just an abstract entity made up of *real* people with minds of their own. If we can change *their* minds, or populate the state with people that believe it is *not* an end in itself, and who believe it must shrink if human flourishing is to grow, then we stand a chance.

3

The Property-Owning Democracy

The beneficent effect upon human character both of the effort to acquire private property and of the opportunity, after it has been acquired, for its wise or foolish use, can hardly be over-estimated . . ., equally fundamental, is the relation between the possession of private property by the people and the stability of the State. . . . So deeply, indeed, has Conservatism felt the importance of this relation that in the past it was wont to maintain that only those who possessed private property should exercise political functions. That doctrine has now this new and pregnant application – that since, today, practically all citizens have political rights, all should possess something of their own.[1] – Noel Skelton

Property and the Good Economy

Who *owns* British society? Such a question would appear irrelevant to someone of the liberal rationalist disposition. The question of property ownership in their worldview is merely incidental; different distributions of capital or property, they would maintain, are as good as each other so long as they advance rather than impede the cause of aggregated economic efficiency.

But property ownership is not of merely incidental relevance to our economic model, and not every distribution of property is conducive to a good society. In fact, a wide distribution of ownership is of *constitutional* importance to our way of life. It ties its structure to a particular moral worldview. It is what enables free economic interactions to serve not just the end of general prosperity but also of personal moral development, and it ensures that the economy as a whole remains plugged into society, of which it forms an important but nonetheless narrow sphere. And it is no exaggeration to say that the values it inculcates are indispensable to a society which aims at the flourishing of its people.

The type of ownership that this book advocates is much broader than the mere ownership of tangible assets. But the distribution of private property is nonetheless an important part of any political economy committed to the values of ownership, for it is the practical means through which those values are learned. And as such, the current trends in property ownership in Britain should be a source of considerable concern.

The Twofold Character of Ownership

Generally, the case for the political significance of property ownership is made at the social or aggregate level – that it has some beneficial effect on the stability or prosperity or cohesiveness of society. Indeed, throughout the history of political thought back to classical antiquity, thinkers have recognised a vital relationship between property ownership and particular types of political order. Such a view is to be found in the work of Aristotle. On the possession of property in general, 'it is impossible', he wrote, 'or at least not easy, to play a noble part unless furnished with the necessary equipment'.[2] More specifically, Aristotle's conception of the good polity – one that contributed to general human flourishing – was one populated with private property owners.

The most stable and durable states are those in which the citizenry 'own a middle or adequate amount of property', he wrote in *Politics*, for this would ensure such a society's balance.[3]

This Aristotelian conception of the importance of property is latent in the republican tradition that John Pocock wrote extensively about, and which tied aptitude for political participation to property ownership.[4] What these republican thinkers recognised is that private property has a profound impact on a person's political psychology. Critically, property gives the owner a material sense of stake in society – a literal investment in its fortunes as inextricably related to his or her own. And it is specifically personal property ownership which has this effect. 'What is held in common', wrote Aristotle, 'receives the least care: For people give most attention to their own property, less to what is communal'.[5]

They also understood there to be a vital connection between the distribution of property and freedom from central authority. The existence of a critical mass of self-sufficient people with independent means would stand as a bulwark against coercion and serve to check or balance governmental power. Finally, there was an intuition that private property had a powerful effect upon the incentives for industry and enterprise. By providing a stable store of value, it enables people to capture the fruits of their economic activities – be it the deployment of their labour or capital – and thus creates a stimulus for productivity.

From a personalist perspective, however, the justification for private property is not first and foremost to be made at the social, but the personal level. The effects of property ownership on the individual are intrinsically valuable. It offers the basic medium through which people might grow and develop as moral characters; it 'grafts benevolence even upon avarice'; and it nurtures in the individual a propensity to exercise responsibility in life – to care for and improve.[6] For one, property constitutes an extension of the self, and the ownership of it an opportunity to cultivate personality. As William James put it:

> the Empirical Self of each of us is all that he is tempted to call by the name me. But it is clear that between what a man calls me and what he simply calls mine the line is difficult to draw. We feel and act about certain things that are ours very much as we feel and act about ourselves . . . In its widest possible sense . . . a man's Self is the sum total of all that he CAN call his.[7]

But this does not render ownership solely self-regarding. Private property also serves as a moral school. It teaches the owner, as Benjamin Disraeli recognised, that rights and opportunities carry corresponding duties.[8] That while one is free to alter their property and derive benefit from it, they are also to bear responsibility for its future liabilities. Private property thus starts not with a promise but a 'demand, a moral appeal'.[9] And in this, the 'paradox' of personal ownership is to be found. That despite the fact that private property annexes itself to the individual, it is the basic life force of communities both local and national. It provides a unifying cause and sense of a shared stake which demands that the individual treats the interest of a given collective as in some way her or his own.

This is the very opposite of communal responsibility or ownership by all. For what everyone owns, nobody owns in an intimate or personal way, and so instead of providing an opportunity for the expression of human character and the taking of responsibility, communal ownership submerges the human person and destroys a sense of obligation. This is the basic deficiency with socialist theories of ownership: in practice, they deny people the autonomy and responsibility which constitutes the main impulse of their desire to own property.

Private ownership connects the free economy to a personalist moral worldview, then. Its principal justification is that it helps to create a sphere for the individual human to exercise free agency, and to take responsibility – the two basic requirements for moral development. But from this follows immense benefits for society more generally. By enabling individuals to flourish, property ownership makes for more cohesive communities populated by people with a real sense of stake and obligation to others, as well as more dynamic economies because of the incentives for work and entrepreneurship it creates. By supporting human flourishing, private property thus promotes the vitality of the economy and society in general.

And the form of community that property has the most pronounced effect upon is also the most human and proximate; that is, the family. The acquisition of property and its passing on gives the identity of the family unit a stability through time – a sense of transgenerational belonging and rootedness, as well as a material stability and security in the present. As such, property helps to perpetuate that form of community which has always provided the primary setting for human flourishing.

Catholic Social Teaching, Distributism and Constructive Conservatism

The beneficent effects of private property at both the individual and social level, however, are *conditional.* They depend on its wide distribution throughout the body politic, and on a set of values and dispositions which temper its exercise. For it is this that makes ownership unifying rather than divisive, enables the flourishing of the many rather than the few, and creates resilient and vibrant communities, rather than pulling them apart. It is when property ownership is widespread, and when it is seen to carry both rights *and* responsibilities, that it serves as a sturdy base for the social structure, and its values become a form of moral cement for the community.

This vital point was best articulated by a series of thinkers who wrote about ownership in the late nineteenth and early twentieth centuries, and it is worth dwelling on this understudied strain of thought for a moment. At the time, and with the transformative effects of industrialisation being felt in societies across Europe and America, considerable angst emerged about the prospects of property ownership in a society increasingly divided into wage-earners and capital owners. In that context, a grave imbalance was opening up between the interests of the propertied and the propertyless.

Equally troublingly, the way of life of which the ideal of property ownership was representative – that rooted in the personal and local, based upon self-provision and moral responsibility – was increasingly under threat from processes that were accelerating the 'massification' of society. In the large scale and impersonal, in the democratised and standardised, individuals were losing their unique identities and characteristics, and becoming subsumed within a social structure that increasingly found it difficult to treat them as inherently valuable. In many ways, it was a period which manifested those social tendencies precipitated by liberal rationalism discussed earlier: the dislocation, atomisation and eventual instrumentalisation of the human person within society.

It was in fact the Catholic Church that first saw in the wide distribution of property ownership a potential response to both these socio-economic problems. In 1891, Pope Leo XIII issued his Papal Encyclical on labour and capital – *Rerum Novarum*. In it, he recognised the revolutionary change wrought by the advent of mass society: its tendency to leave men and women 'broken in spirit and worn down in body', the 'changed relations between masters and workmen', and the development of 'enormous fortunes of some few individuals, and the utter poverty of the masses'.[10]

But Pope Leo rejected the case made by socialism – that the communal ownership of property by the state would address the divisions between workers and existing owners and give individuals a renewed sense of belonging and identity. He argued that their proposed remedy was worse than the disease, because it deprived the wage-earner both of 'all hope and possibility of increasing his resources and of bettering his condition in life', as well as his natural right to freely pursue his own moral development:

> The door would be thrown open to envy, to mutual invective, and to discord; the sources of wealth themselves would run dry, for no one would have any interest in exerting his talents or his industry; and that ideal equality about which they entertain pleasant dreams would be in reality the levelling down of all to a like condition of misery and degradation.[11]

'Hence', he continued,

> it is clear that the main tenet of socialism, community of goods, must be utterly rejected, since it only injures those whom it would seem meant to benefit, is directly contrary to the natural rights of mankind, and would introduce confusion and disorder into the commonweal.[12]

At the most fundamental level, Leo argued, the socialist worldview could not be acceptable to the Christian worldview, because it failed to recognise the inherent dignity of the human individual. 'The first and most fundamental principle, therefore, if one would undertake to alleviate the condition of the masses, must be the inviolability of private property', because it is through property that we gain the opportunity to develop morally. And so, government should 'favour ownership, and its policy should be to induce as many as possible of the people to become owners'.[13]

'Inviolability' did not imply absoluteness for Leo, and he argued that property rights were limited by the very nature of man as possessing inherent dignity and value. For him, this demanded that 'duties' towards others were observed in the exercise of private property. Private property gained its legitimacy as an institution through its conformity with the Christian moral universe.

Extending property ownership more widely, he continued, would bring classes of people closer together, improve economic productivity – 'as men always work harder and more readily when they work on that which belongs to them' – and also increase people's sense of stake in their country (people would 'cling' more closely to their country, he wrote).

But it was not a quantitative distribution that mattered, so much as a *qualitative* one – that more people should have ownership of something, not that all people should own equally. It is 'impossible to reduce civil society to one dead level', however much 'socialists may in that intent do their utmost'. 'There naturally exist among mankind manifold differences of the most important kind; people differ in capacity, skill, health, strength; and unequal fortune is a necessary result of unequal condition.'[14] And so the responsibility of government was not to equalise the amount of property that people own, but to give as many people as possible the opportunity of being an owner.

Pope Leo offered a remarkably coherent case for the wide diffusion of property as a means of combatting the irresponsibility of liberal rationalism and the threat of statist domination. And it was a case that was developed by the distributists in the early twentieth century, the two most prominent exponents of which were Hilaire Belloc and G. K. Chesterton. Belloc's essay on *The Servile State* is perhaps the best exemplar of the distributist thesis. An English Catholic himself, Belloc identified a similar economic problem to that which Pope Leo observed: a society divided between 'possessors' and 'non-possessors' that produced 'severe strains' arising from the 'divergence between the moral theories upon which the state reposes and the social facts which those moral theories attempt to govern', and 'from the insecurity to which capitalism condemns the great mass of society, and the general character of anxiety and peril which it imposes on all citizens, but in particular upon the majority, which consists . . . of dispossessed free men'.[15]

In these circumstances, Belloc contended, with property owned by too narrow a portion of the population, society was in a state of imbalance or 'disequilibrium', and would seek stable equilibrium either through the wide diffusion of property, or in the form of what he calls the 'Servile State' – an arrangement in which people become divided into free capital owners and unfree proletarians who work for a guaranteed return but who lose the right to withdraw their labour.

Belloc worried that Britain was 'drifting' towards the latter situation. Socialists who aimed at the ideal of collective ownership were merely fostering another form of economic oligarchy and thus servility. But equally as significant in this drift was the psychological effects that the deprivation of property had upon the masses, whose insecurity and dependency made them particularly receptive to the idea of something or someone else providing for their wants and needs:

> The first effect is this: that property is no longer what they seek, nor what they think obtainable for themselves. The second effect is that they regard the possessors of property as a class apart, whom they always must ultimately obey, often envy and sometimes hate . . . the attitude of the proletariat in England today . . . towards property and towards that freedom which is alone obtainable through property is no longer an attitude of experience or of expectation. They think of themselves as wage earners. To increase the weekly stipend of the wage earner is an object which they vividly appreciate and pursue. To make him cease to be a wage earner is an object that would seem to them entirely outside the realities of life.[16]

Restricted property ownership, Belloc argued, created forms of insecurity and dependency that would diminish a people's vitality, foment jealousies that threaten social cohesion, and generate demand for a supervisory power that could relieve people of the need to take responsibility for their own lives. But

Belloc did not believe these trends were inherent in modernity, or a necessary consequence of the vast increase in productive capacity brought on by industrialisation. It was, rather, the 'deliberate action of men, evil will in a few and apathy of will among the many', that had left so many without the security and self-sufficiency that derives from property. 'It was not machinery that lost us our freedom; it was the loss of a free mind'.[17]

Nevertheless, the iteration of this distributist doctrine most familiar to a British audience is that put forward by Noel Skelton in his writings on 'Constructive Conservatism' in the aftermath of the Great War. Like Belloc, Skelton recognised the instability of a society transformed by industrialisation and increasingly polarised by the uneven distribution of property. In addition, the advent of mass democracy and universal education had intensified this instability, he contended, because it meant that, although the 'mass of the people' had become politically and intellectually enfranchised, they remained economically disenfranchised and insecure. As a result, the social structure had become 'lopsided'. The 'master problem of the new era' was to restore society's balance.[18]

Skelton also rejected the solution proposed by socialism. He recognised the intellectual and emotional force of the socialist case, for it appealed to the deep instinctive desire of people for a stake in society and the security that property provides. But in advocating for communal ownership through the state, the socialist only perverted those impulses:

> he declares that ownership by the State is ownership by the people, implying that that means a property-owning democracy. In fact, of course, it does not. What everybody owns, nobody owns; and far from expressing the wage-earner's ideal, Socialism makes it unattainable, while communal ownership, when obtained, neither interests nor influences a single human being. We have yet to hear of the man who, in the Great War, rushed

> to arms to preserve his share in the London County Council Tramways or in Battersea Park.[19]

To make democracy truly 'stable and four-square', Skelton argued, it was necessary 'to give the wage-earner property and status; to bridge the gulf set between Labour and Capital'. To build, in other words, a 'property-owning democracy', whereby as many people as possible were afforded the opportunity of acquiring property and the values that come with it.

Skelton considered this project to be quintessentially conservative. The property-owning democracy was a blueprint for safeguarding 'the stability of the social structure':

> A stable condition of society is the main pre-occupation of Conservatism . . . for, as the generations come and go, the opportunity offered for full enjoyment and full development to each individual during his little span of consciousness depends upon the society and community which surrounds and contains him being stable.[20]

It was also the means through which those basic values which support a prosperous and flourishing society might be encouraged and disseminated:

> the character of the individual citizen being the greatest asset of the State, the primary object and best test of all legislation which deals with the individual is its influence upon his character. Everything that weakens individual character and lessens individual effort and initiative is anathema to the Conservative. Everything that strengthens and increases these is very near to his heart. The consequences flowing from this principle need no elaboration here. Enough to say that the main and most essential one is the insistence by Conservatism on the necessity of limiting the action of the State to 'helping the individual to help himself'.[21]

The property-owning democracy, Skelton averred, was the means of securing these two conservative objects. 'Mocked and jeered at in the past as "the Party of Property", it is precisely as such, now that the wheel has turned full circle, that Conservatism in the new era holds in its keeping the key to the problem.'

The policy implications of Skelton's ideas were highly radical; he called for 'co-partnery' (profit sharing) and employee share ownership schemes in order to render capital and labour 'partners in the . . . production of wealth', as well as a drastic expansion of smallholdings, inspired by the land reforms pursued by Conservative governments in Ireland via the Wyndham Land Act.

In Skelton, then, we have the fullest articulation of the case for the diffuse ownership of property, and its function in a society committed to the flourishing of its people. Property ownership represented a 'practical medium for the expression of moral and intellectual qualities', an educator in responsibility, and a source of freedom for the owner. It was the vital integrative and stabilising force in the social structure, giving owners a stake in their local and wider community, and when widely distributed, a unifying moral and ethical framework. It offered not just security, but a *real*, self-sufficient security, as opposed to that provided at the discretion of others. In all of this, it would underpin a society in which people flourished. In so doing, wide property ownership would also create the incentives and inducements for productivity, dynamism and economic 'progress' – the sort of progress 'which the State cannot dole out with a spoon'.[22]

The Narrowing of Ownership

Skelton and the distributists before him set out an ideal that was in deep conformity with the inherited moral and ethical values of the British people. It was one that would in different ways be adopted and repackaged by subsequent political entrepreneurs throughout the twentieth century.[23] Yet in recent years, our society has moved further and further away from that vision of a property-owning democracy. Of course, our culture today is permeated by the wide ownership of consumer goods – of cars, watches, mobile phones, laptops and so on. But this is merely a distraction from the fact that ownership of those assets which comprise the nation's true wealth is becoming less widespread. A vast narrowing of the number of owners has taken place, with an attendant diminution in the values which property ownership incapsulates.

Of course, the part of the economy where this is most evident is in the housing market. Homes are the first form of asset that individuals and households aspire to own. They provide the most basic sense of security – a place of refuge and privacy, a setting for the formation of families, a source of stability in bricks and stone. In the decades after the Second World War, the number of households that owned their home increased precipitously, particularly as a result of the vast transfer of housing assets from state ownership into private hands through the 'Right to Buy' policy, whereby council tenants could buy their home at a discount. Indeed, this was the main driver of increased home ownership in the period. Housebuilding rates – the generation of new housing units for owner-occupancy – were actually on a decidedly downwards trajectory from 1947 onwards.[24] And while Right to Buy was a successful means of promoting home ownership, its efficacy was finite and limited to the existing stock of state-owned housing.

Home ownership thus peaked in the early 2000s. Since then, it has been on a downward trajectory, falling by about 7 per cent across the entire population. But it is trends in younger demographics that are of most acute concern. Since the 1990s, the home ownership rate for those aged between 25 and 34 – precisely the age that people wish to be starting families and taking on real responsibility in their personal and professional lives – has fallen by about a third.

This decline in ownership has not been driven by a lack of demand among young people. Studies show that millennials aspire to home ownership just as much as their parents did.[25] Rather, it is the result of accelerating unaffordability. While at the start of the century a house was roughly four times annual earnings for the average person, it is now over eight times.

The situation is even worse in cities like London, where the average house price is more like *thirteen* times the average income. Given that lenders will generally only provide credit for around four to five times annual earnings, this means that home ownership is virtually unattainable for the vast majority of young people, unless they are in the very highest-earning percentiles, or are inheriting a vast amount of wealth. In other words, that generation of young people that is coming of age, and to whom our society will look for the future leaders of our businesses, communities and political institutions, is entering a world in which the most intuitive aspirational ideal known to our way of life is increasingly out of reach.

Beyond the housing market, the trends are the same. The number of British households with direct equity holdings has been on a long-term downward trend, despite efforts in the 1980s to stimulate share ownership. The number of households directly owning stocks and shares has halved between 2004 and 2022.[26] Since 1963, the proportion of British shares owned by individuals has fallen by over 40 percentage points from 54 per cent to 12 per cent. Almost 60 per cent of British stocks are owned by foreign investors.

Though it is certainly true that many individuals own shares indirectly through their pensions, the proportion of UK listed equities owned by British pension funds has collapsed from around 30 per cent in the 1990s to roughly 2 per cent. In other words, British business and industry is increasingly owned by overseas investors and institutions who may well lack a sense of long-term stake in these companies.

More generally, public markets in the UK are on the decline as companies opt to remain private. There has been a drop of around 75 per cent in the number of businesses listed on the London Stock Exchange since the 1960s, and around 25 per cent in the last decade alone. And these trends have been even more pronounced among smaller listed companies – those with less than £10.2 million annual turnover.[27] The number of such companies has dropped by nearly a third, and the number of new issues had fallen by 80 per cent.[28]

Even when opportunities for property ownership are extended, the form they take is thinner and more distant from the sort of relationships that foster responsibility and a genuine sense of stake. Retail share ownership platforms should be an opportunity for a vast expansion of genuine ownership in the British economy. Instead, take-up is low, and the type of personality it encourages is the transient speculator rather than the invested owner. As we saw earlier, private companies too often treat ownership not as a responsibility which comes with long-term obligations, but as a means for extracting short-term value. New homes are not designed to be durable investments in a particular place for their future owners, but financial assets that can earn a return.

For those of the liberal rationalist persuasion, it might be enough simply to afford people the opportunities of owning while trying to minimise the responsibilities that are their necessary counterpart. But that is not enough for a society built to last.

Economic Infantilisation

The damaging consequences of all of this can be observed at an aggregate level. Economically, concentrated property ownership leaves many without assets and consequently more dependent on credit and exposed to inflationary spikes. It also reduces labour market flexibility – because without assets to fall back on, workers are less willing to take risks by switching jobs, or indeed starting a business of their own – and diminishes the incentives for industry and enterprise furnished by the prospect of acquiring capital. More obliquely, narrowing property ownership is related to the low levels of investment that will be discussed in the next chapter, and which are a key reason for the UK's poor productivity growth.

Socially, the concentration of property transforms ownership from an integrative, aspirational ideal into a contentious symbol of inequity. It is even undermining the social function of the family, both directly – as fewer younger households are able to acquire the sort of residential property that provides the best setting for raising children – and indirectly – as that desire to pass something on to future generations becomes perverted into some sort of exclusive privilege of the few rather than the natural instinct of the many.

Nevertheless, the truly deleterious trends that this narrowing of ownership is generating are taking place at the personal level. It is evident in the growing sense among the propertyless that they are distant or detached from the economy – or more precisely that the economy has become detached from them. That their economic fortunes are not really in their own gift but are subject to decisions and actions outside of their control. Most importantly, the decline of property ownership is feeding a sense that responsibility is something to be avoided, something to be outsourced to others. The propertyless are increasingly dependent on a particular level of income to sustain their present consumption, which makes them more risk-averse, and more willing for the state to intervene in the economy to guarantee their wages and the security of their employment.

We see this cultural shift in the growing proportion of people employed by large corporations and indeed by the state itself, in the increasing regulation of the labour market, and finally, in the growing financial liabilities being incurred by the state as it becomes responsible for the present and future security of individuals. What is occurring as a result of thinning property ownership, in other words, is the economic and social *infantilisation* of the British public, as people growing into adulthood are first deprived of the chance to become responsible members of society and then are conditioned to fear the very prospect of that responsibility. That very infantilisation generates demand for a supervisory, 'tutelary' power in the form of the state, which can only guarantee people's consumption and security through measures that drain the vital energies upon which economic prosperity depends.

Here then, we see clearly the relationship between reduced personal independence deriving from the concentration of property ownership, the augmented demand for state security that follows, and the debilitating consequences of all this for the economy. Perversely, we have been taught to welcome rising asset prices as a driver of economic growth, because it improves the confidence of existing owners and their willingness to consume. But that is a deeply misguided view if it diminishes the incentives for work and enterprise of non-owners by making property ownership more unaffordable, if it leaves more households economically insecure and dependent on external support, and if it contributes to a burgeoning state that draws more and more on the resources of the productive parts of the economy.

Conservative Handmaidens

Specific failings in government have hastened this concentration in property ownership, none more so than in the housing market. For decades, our country has failed to deliver a sufficient number of new homes, while loosening credit conditions to make it easier to borrow. The result has been deteriorating affordability, but also distortions in the wider economy that have gone largely unseen.

The broad context for this failing is a statist planning framework which demands that explicit permission from government be secured whenever a new home is to be built. This discretionary system has created uncertainty for housebuilders, raised the cost of developable land and over time introduced vast regulatory or bureaucratic costs to the process of gaining permission for and actually building a new home. But it has also dragged decision-making about how communities are to change or grow and develop away from local people. The result has been that smaller developers have been squeezed out of the market, the number of new homes delivered has fallen, the quality of those homes has deteriorated considerably, and all the while affordability has become worse and worse.

Philosophically, we have come to see property not as a moral opportunity that ought to be extended to as many people as possible, but an investment good, the real value of which must be constantly bid upwards for the sake of the macro economy. And in practice, government policies – both Labour and Conservative – have advanced the interests of existing property owners *at the expense* of aspirant ones. In certain regards they have tightened the restrictions on new development while running a loose monetary policy of low interest rates and easy access to mortgage finance (not to mention a loose immigration policy, which shall be considered later).

While that has enabled some individuals and families to become homeowners in the short run, it has made for a vastly more unaffordable market in the long term, as an increasing volume of money chases a finite number of houses. All of this has been to the benefit of the propertied, as the value of their asset has soared. But it has rendered the aspiration to own a home unattainable for great swathes of the population.

The electoral consequences for the Conservative Party of these developments have been momentous. Conservatives have long recognised that owners tend to develop a political psychology conducive to its creed – a belief in personal responsibility, in freedom, a respect for the value of money, a sense of stake in the broader community. But in failing to propagate new generations of homeowners, Conservatives have lately restricted themselves to an electorate composed merely of those who already own.

What is often overlooked is the knock-on effects that this has for other forms of property ownership. A home of one's own remains the first and most natural object of ownership – the most tangible stake in society that a household can secure for themselves. And it is thus the case that many will choose to hold off acquiring other forms of property until they build the capital required to finance the purchase of a home. But if house prices are rising and the deposit required for a home purchase is correspondingly rising too, and such increases are occurring more quickly than earnings, that means that people are taking longer to be in a position to buy a home and are therefore delaying the point at which they acquire other assets like stocks or shares. The decline in home ownership has not seen a corresponding rise in share ownership, which suggests that the effects of unaffordability in the housing market is having diffuse impacts across the economy.

Even then, people who are not accumulating the capital for a home purchase – those who might not wish to be homeowners or perhaps existing homeowners – are holding onto cash and opting not to acquire stocks or shares, even when the real value of that cash is eroding over time. People do not *want* to become owners; they don't want the risk and liability that comes with being responsible for something of value.

These dynamics have all been sustained by a monetary policy that has bolstered the prices of a range of assets from equities to residential real estate, but which has also undercut the purchasing power of people's earnings. It might feel good in the short term to be able to acquire property through cheaper borrowing. But with more money chasing the same number of goods, the inevitable result is inflation, which serves in the long run to transfer wealth from earners to the already propertied.

The Error of Redistribution

These are all relatively proximate causes of the decline of property ownership in this country – ways in which government policies have hindered rather than advanced the cause of wider property ownership in particular parts of the economy. But they are symptomatic of a much broader trend within our political culture – one which places far less value upon property ownership.

Our liberal rationalist culture sees the economy as a self-supporting piece of machinery, which if managed correctly by technicians can ensure a sufficient level of output to sustain the lifestyles of those who participate in it. From this perspective, property ownership can quite easily come to be seen not as an inviolable principle of the economic system itself, but as a *problem* from the perspective of the economic technician, since it disperses power and control.

In the past, the common response proffered by property's opponents was to centralise and collectivise the ownership of property in the hands of the state. But today, and with the failed experiments in collectivised ownership at least faintly in the consciousness of the economic technicians, the scheme most frequently proposed is that of social democracy: to compensate for the unbalanced distribution of property ownership through fiscal redistribution.

The argument is to be found articulated in diverse ways, but its contemporary exemplar is to be found in the work of Thomas Piketty. The key thesis advanced by Piketty in his *Capital in the Twenty-First Century* is that, over the long run, returns to capital outpace economic growth, and as such the share of the income or wealth generated in a year accruing to capital will grow at the expense of that directed to labour.

It is this wealth inequality which perturbs Piketty, rather than the narrow ownership of capital, for in that inequality he sees the seeds of economic crises driven by the inefficiencies of weak demand and reduced purchasing power. His remedy for unequal ownership of capital is a vastly expanded level of taxation on both incomes and on capital itself, and he is willing to accept a profound increase in the overall tax burden in the process. The rationalistic underpinnings of his thesis are overt:

> In theory there is no reason why a country cannot decide to devote *two thirds or three quarters* of its national income to taxes, assuming that taxes are collected in a transparent and efficient manner and used for purposes that everyone agrees are of high priority, such as education, health, culture, clean energy, and sustainable development. Taxation is neither good nor bad in itself. Everything depends on how taxes are collected and what they are used for.[29]

The narrowing of property ownership in this country has created fertile soil for such ideas to take hold. If property is something that *others* own, it is altogether easier to call for it to be taxed more aggressively. If you are a beneficiary of or dependent on state largesse in one form or another, through your employment or through state expenditure, you have a vested interest in the state's revenues being augmented. If you have come to believe that the rights of existing property owners come at the expense of your own ability to pursue a better future for yourself or for your family, then you are unlikely to be moved by the complaints of those who observe their existing wealth being eroded.

There are already concerns about the data Piketty uses to justify his claim.[30] On its own terms, however, and from the perspective of the efficiency of the economy, his proposed solution is futile. If, as Piketty suggests, there is an inherent logic to the accumulation of capital which means that a constantly increasing share of wealth is directed towards it, then logically it follows that the rate of progressive taxation required to compensate for the inequality in property ownership will grow accordingly. That escalating tax burden – especially if it reaches the marginal rates advocated by Piketty – will diminish the incentives not only to work but also to take the investment risks that will boost the productive capacity of the economy and thus overall living standards.

But these concerns are of second-order importance. The more fundamental flaw is that fiscal redistribution does not at all address the root issue, which is the distribution of *property*. Indeed, higher rates of tax inevitably hit those in a position to accumulate capital and leave them with less disposable income to deploy in acquiring assets or setting up a business. Instead of aiding the hard-working and aspirant to achieve their basic desire for a real stake in the economy and a source of self-sufficiency, redistribution renders those aspirations increasingly unattainable.

At the same time, there is strong evidence to suggest that the phenomenon that Piketty identifies – of returns to capital outpacing those to labour – is almost entirely the consequence of efforts to *constrain* the wider distribution of property. The rise in the value of capital he charts is to a significant extent accounted for by the capital gains on dwellings and land, which is driven principally by government regulation and loose monetary policy. In other words, inequality has little to do with inherent dynamics in capital. It has everything to do with destructive efforts to prevent ownership becoming more widely distributed, and an approach to the money supply intended to sustain present levels of spending and consumption.[31]

All of this corrodes the very idea of property itself. Rather than being the principal institution of a society committed to the personal development of its people, property becomes a temporary, precarious gift bestowed by the state which can be whittled away at its discretion. Indeed, advocates of so-called 'Modern Monetary Theory' contend that the property taxed by government does not even really belong to the owner at all, jumping from the banal observation that governments are needed to facilitate market economies to the conclusion that the state is therefore the primary economic agent: 'Tax is not taxpayers money', Richard Murphy writes in *The Joy of Tax*; 'it is the government's money and it is the government's rightful property. It is absurd to claim otherwise.'[32] The purpose of tax, Murphy continues, 'is to reorganise the economy to ensure it delivers the government's economic goals'.[33]

But in a world in which property can be taxed to an ever-escalating degree in order to pursue objectives set at the social level, property ceases to be a source of independence and self-sufficiency, and can no longer anchor the economy to a way of life rooted in the belief that people should be responsible and in control of their own lives. And so society's centre of gravity continues to shift upwards towards the state and away from the personal sphere.

The Restoration of Property

Preserving in aspic the distribution of ownership in British society while confiscating the proceeds of wealth and redistributing them to sustain aggregate demand is a totally inadequate response to the structural maladies of our economy. Instead, 'the redemption of the non-owning workers' should be our goal – such that the aspirant too might acquire property, and with it the opportunity and security that it provides.[34]

What our country now needs is the 'restoration of property' – a programme for reestablishing property as a vital source of independence and for effecting a vast diffusion of ownership throughout British society. Critically, these two objects must be pursued simultaneously; the distribution of property must not be achieved by compulsorily taking from some to give to others, but by multiplying the opportunities for people to become owners. It will require a proactive government committed to shaping the values of its people, but also one dedicated to pushing down decision-making authority back towards the personal level.

The significance of this programme should not be underestimated. It amounts to a total reversal of governing policy in the post-war period. It will be exceptionally difficult to persuade the Treasury in its current composition, for example, of the merits of investing resources into spreading property ownership without the expectation of a return for the government. Yet far from earning a return, the way we currently raise taxes and spend them is harming the ultimate sources of both prosperity and government revenues. Property distribution is a risk, but it is a risk that will pay long-term dividends. Continuing down the current path in which a higher and higher tax burden is required to offset concentrated property ownership promises certain stagnation.

Not all forms of property ownership will yield the same pecuniary returns. But that really is a second-order issue. The object sought is not an equalisation of wealth, but a multiplication of the number of people who own *something*, and who thus have the chance to develop the moral and political psychology that comes with ownership.

But if wider property ownership is the end sought, the environment in which this will be made possible is one where more people have managed to save sufficient capital, and where they are provided sufficient incentives to do so. This is the subject of the next chapter.

4

Savings, Investment and the Intergenerational Contract

Society is, indeed, a contract . . . It is to be looked on with reverence; because it is not a partnership in things subservient only to the gross animal existence of a temporary and perishable nature. It is a partnership in all science, a partnership in all art, a partnership in every virtue and in all perfection. As the ends of such a partnership cannot be obtained in many generations, it becomes a partnership not only between those who are living, but between those who are living, those who are dead, and those who are to be born.[1] – Edmund Burke

The bourgeoisie worked primarily in order to invest, and it was not so much a standard of consumption as a standard of accumulation that the bourgeoisie struggled for and tried to defend against governments that took the short-run view. With the decline of the driving power supplied by the family motive, the businessman's time horizons shrink, roughly to his life expectation. And he might now be less willing than he was to fulfil that function of earning, saving and investing . . . He drifts into an anti-saving frame of mind and accepts with an increasing readiness anti-saving theories that are indicative of a short-run philosophy.[2] – Joseph Schumpeter

Consumptionism

An important counterpart to the liberal rationalist economic worldview is what I propose to call the ethic of consumptionism.[3] Proponents of consumptionism would certainly be loath to describe it as an 'ethic'. The fundamental basis of their view is that economics itself is non-ethical; not immoral, but *amoral* – concerned with the 'form' but not the 'substance' of economic behaviour. Economics is, as Lionel Robbins once put it, 'in no way to be conceived as we may conceive Ethics or Aesthetics as being concerned with ends as such'.[4] For Benedetto Croce, economics concerned the practical activities of men 'emptied of all content, moral or immoral'.[5] It is interested not in the ends sought, but the utility of certain actions in achieving particular ends. This conception of economics as non-moral is partly the upshot of attempts by practising economists to establish the scientific bona fides of their discipline. But it also derives from a tendency in other quarters to relegate the economic sphere to some lower level of human endeavour.

Of course, the idea that economics can ever be unconcerned with ends is illusory. The end of utility is still an end, after all. In an economy emptied of moral content, the purpose of activity becomes the maximisation of the consumption of goods and services in the here and now. Individuals are transformed from multidimensional, relational beings into one-dimensional consumers, concerned above all else with satisfying their own desires. It is a distinctly liberal vision, because – at least at first – it leaves each individual to pursue whatever most satisfies their wants and proclivities.

But it is also a decidedly rationalist view too, since it considers consumption the fuel or sustenance of the economic machine, and the maximisation of consumption as a fundamentally technical question. As Hannah Arendt wrote, there is 'nothing more at stake' in the economic realm 'than labouring and consuming, which obviously are the lowest and most compulsory of all human activities'.[6]

Consumptionism as I am defining it should not be confused with a proper understanding of the economic concept of consumption. Adam Smith famously wrote that 'consumption is the sole end and purpose of all production; and the interest of the producer ought to be attended to, only so far as it may be necessary for promoting that of the consumer'.[7] His vital point was that production and consumption are two sides of the same coin, and that *value* is created only when something is produced that someone genuinely wants to consume. Production for production's sake will not make us more prosperous.

The consumptionist ethic is something of a perversion of this basic insight. It holds first that consumption *now* – the immediate satisfaction of *present* demand – is the highest object to be achieved. And in its demoralised vision of the economy, it considers all forms of consumption to be equally valid and worthy. In this, consumptionism deviates considerably from the Smithian vision of the economy as embedded in a system of shared 'moral sentiments', and in which 'parsimony' is 'the immediate cause of the increase of capital'.[8] Instead, consumptionism is of a piece with the liberal rationalist strain of thought that has been examined in this book, since it treats economics as a separate domain to society, and thus unconnected to a broader moral view of life.

Consumptionism holds that expanding, maintaining and increasing the efficiency of present consumption is the highest objective of all economic policy. To achieve this, wages need to be guaranteed at a particular level to ensure purchasing power; prices need to be low and stable; the workforce needs to be fully employed; imports need to be cheap; and risk needs to be excised from household and business investment decisions, from labour markets, and from the business cycle.

At their disposal, economic technicians have a range of tools with which to tinker and fine-tune the economic machine to maximise consumption levels. They can redistribute spending power through the taxation system. They can directly boost spending in the economy to head off unemployment. They can make debt cheaper. They can have the government borrow more money and spend it on behalf of the citizenry. They can use monetary policy to inflate the value of assets or affect the price of currency. They can try to regulate away risk. And they can, as will be explored in a later chapter, feed more people into the economy through immigration.

In recent times, policymakers have used these instruments prodigiously. Government expenditure has increased to consume a greater proportion of the economy. Net immigration has grown from around 160,00 in the year to June 2012 to a peak of over 900,000 in 2023 – a number of people roughly equal to the population of Nottingham. The UK's regulatory burden has continued to grow despite commitments from successive governments to the contrary. Before the 2022 inflationary shocks in international energy prices, the Bank of England's base rate – the rate at which the central bank pays commercial banks to hold deposits with it, and which therefore largely determines the rate at which commercial banks charge people to borrow or pay on their savings – had been on a decidedly downward trajectory since the 1990s, and hovered just above zero for the thirteen years after the Great Financial Crisis. The upshot has been that despite recessions, supply shocks, conflicts and pandemics, consumption levels have, with a few blips, been largely maintained.

Consumer confidence and consumption has prevented the economy from completely stalling, despite weak performance across so many other metrics. But ultimately, the proactive efforts by government to sustain consumption has been a double-edged sword, and in many regards are to blame for Britain's weak productivity growth. And in privileging consumption as the only end to be sought in economic decision-making, policymakers have in fact undermined the fundamental sources of prosperity. Most importantly, consumptionism has eroded people's sense of stake and responsibility in delivering shared prosperity, and in treating people as mere recipients or consumers, it has depersonalised them and diminished their capacity for lives of meaning and flourishing.

Prosperity and the Intergenerational Contract

In his *Reflections on the Revolution in France*, Edmund Burke famously described society as a compact – 'a partnership in all science, a partnership in all art, a partnership in every virtue and in all perfection'. The ends of these partnerships, he wrote, could not be achieved in one generation, and thus the partnership upon which he believed society to be based was intergenerational – 'between those who are living, those who are dead, and those who are to be born'.[9]

We might think of prosperity as one of those partnerships the fruits of which are attained over many generations. Economic activity takes place through and across time, and while consumption may well be its purpose, the point at which a good or service is consumed comes at the end of an extended process in which a demand is identified, resources are allocated for production, risk is taken, the product is distributed, and so on. To have access to abundant energy today, for example, or to the roads we use to transport ourselves, or the homes we live in, even to the high-quality goods we enjoy, we rely on economic decisions taken long ago. And likewise, future generations will rely on decisions we make today for their own quality of life.

Economically, the past, present and future are connected through the processes of saving and investment, lending and borrowing. Out of the resources or income available to a person, some proportion will be spent or deployed in the present – to address basic needs, or in response to immediate demands, or for enjoyment. But some portion will not be utilised immediately. It will be saved, implicitly to be used or enjoyed in the future – either by the individual or perhaps by a loved one. These savings are then made available to the capital market and influence the amount of capital that can be extended as credit.

The entrepreneur or business person's role in the market is to identify a demand that isn't currently being met and to satisfy it – or to take an existing product or service and deliver it more effectively. To do this, they often borrow money from banks or raise capital by offering equity to institutional investors or individual savers.[10] They use these funds to invest in new factories, machinery, training or other forms of capital. If the business succeeds, it sells goods or services for more than it costs to produce them. The difference – the profit – is the reward for taking the risk and meeting a demand.

This investment process, whereby savings are deployed to improve the productive capacity of the economy, is the engine of improved prosperity. It is what enables us to produce more things of value for the same amount of resource or – what amounts to the same thing – to produce the same thing for a lower price, thus driving up living standards. It is what propels the innovation process – enabling us to solve problems or bring new products of value to market. And it is what delivers the infrastructure that we all rely upon too.

That willingness to defer the satisfaction of desires today for gratification further down the line – or indeed for the satisfaction of a child or relative – is no mean feat. 'To abstain from the enjoyment which is in our power', wrote one nineteenth-century economist, 'or to seek distant rather than immediate results, is among the most power exertions of human will.'[11] But it is essential to the process of capital accumulation and thus economic development.

To this end, in a free economy, an inducement is offered to persuade the saver to lend his capital – both to compensate for the risk of it not being returned or diminishing in value over time, and for the opportunity cost of parting temporarily with money (since it can no longer be deployed today). That inducement is *interest* – 'human impatience crystallised in a market rate', as Irving Fisher put it. Edward Chancellor offers a wonderful metaphor for these interactions in his book *The Price of Time*. Imagine, he writes:

> That the present and the future are two countries separated by a river. Finance is the intertemporal bridge that joins them together, connecting the present with the future. By acts of borrowing and lending, and saving and investing, we shift expenditures across time. Interest is the toll levied on borrowers for bringing forward consumption and the fee paid to savers for moving consumption into the future. The level of interest regulates the traffic on the bridge and its general direction. When the interest toll is raised, spending is pushed into the future, and consumption is brought forward when the toll is lowered.[12]

Interest is not in itself productive, but it plays a vital role in the process of lending and credit which *is* productive. By placing a premium on borrowing, it gives a price to risk-taking and so helps to ensure the effective allocation of capital; encourages saving, which affects the amount of capital available for lending; and creates balance between the economic interests of the present and the future. And it is that balance and parity of esteem which binds the generations together, and makes possible the aspiration that those who follow us will enjoy a better life than we do.

Such a perspective on intergenerational obligation is a central component of that *bourgeois* worldview discussed earlier in the book. And it is deeply implicated with the idea of the family. Most people save not merely for their own personal future consumption, but for that of their family – for that of their spouse in retirement, and for their children. It is the family which has historically served the role of extending the time horizons of people further into both the past and the future, both in terms of the debts they owe to those who have come before, and those they owe to those yet to come.

Disownership and Economic Irresponsibility

Consumptionism rejects the importance of that intergenerational balance and parity. It is an ideology of impatience, one willing to use up the reserves of the economy to pay for present operating costs. It is a worldview which champions not the *pursuit* of happiness, but the present enjoyment of happiness. Fundamentally, consumptionism is a political economy of the short term. Its disposition towards the notion of an intergenerational partnership is one of cynicism, a disposition best encapsulated by that famous quotation that 'in the long run we are all dead'.

Keynes, the author of that quotation, was writing in a particular context when he penned those words. But they encapsulate an approach to the economy that is widely held – one which has been decidedly influential in economic policymaking. In abstract terms, our society faces the same basic economic dilemma that any community faces: that is, there is a scarcity of resources available for addressing everyone's wants and needs. In concrete terms, there are too few homes to meet everyone's demand for housing. Demand for social services outstrips our means of paying for them. Our desire for energy – to heat our homes, to power our offices, to build our products – is greater than the quantity of energy we can supply at present. There is not enough national income to meet everyone's wage demands.

A society can respond to this basic, inexorable economic problem in a variety of ways. The more long-term, 'bourgeois' approach is that of capital accumulation. It responds to the problem of scarcity through present restraint in the hope of greater future abundance. It advises that resources should be put aside now to make everyone more prosperous in the future. The alternative, consumptionist response is to shift resources through time in the opposite direction; to take from the future in order to sustain the wants and needs of the present. And it proposes to achieve this first and foremost by borrowing – and making it easier to borrow – from the future.

Our society has gradually shifted away from the bourgeois approach towards the consumptionist one. Firstly, since the 1970s, the previous monetary mechanism which tied credit to foregone consumption has been transformed into one in which banks essentially conjure up credit by issuing loans with corresponding deposits – or as the Bank of England itself put it in 2014, 'rather than banks lending out of deposits placed with them, the act of lending creates deposits'.[13] The link that previously existed between savings and capital has thus been severed. In this specific regard, the modern monetary theorists are correct – indeed, they themselves describe credit as a 'conjuring trick' in this novel system.[14]

The problem is, Modern Monetary Theory is not merely 'descriptive', as Stephanie Kelton puts it; it is also normative – it seeks to justify such a monetary system, and to contend that since the state underwrites all economic activity through issuing currency, it therefore ought to be the principal agent in the economy. Its recommendations are dangerous, because it downplays the very real trade-offs that have to be made in the *real* economy about how resources are employed, and whether they are put towards meeting present demands or increasing future prosperity.

More recently, ultra-low interest rates have been introduced in an attempt to stimulate growth by expanding the amount of credit in the economy and encouraging borrowing. But by making it cheaper to borrow in the here and now, such a monetary policy also discouraged savings and weakened the signals that direct capital towards productive investment. The result has been not an expansion in the productive capacity of the economy, but simply an inflation in the value of existing assets. Households and companies are not investing to increase the total capital stock, but to increase the market value of their existing assets. Which is why house and share prices remain buoyant, while investment languishes.

Ironically, then, loose monetary policy has encouraged higher levels of borrowing, but not increased levels of investment in the parts of the economy that need it. This should not have come as a surprise. As Henry Hazlitt put it almost eighty years ago:

> The effect of keeping interest rates artificially low, in fact, is eventually the same as that of keeping any other price below the natural market. It increases demand and reduces supply. It increases the demand for capital and reduces the supply of real capital. It brings about a scarcity. It creates economic distortions. It is true, no doubt, that an artificial reduction in the interest rate encourages increased borrowing. It tends, in fact, to encourage highly speculative ventures that cannot continue except under the artificial conditions that gave them birth. On the supply side, the artificial reduction of interest rates discourages normal thrift and saving. It brings about a comparative shortage of real capital.[15]

Here, we see two processes taking place which have been immensely damaging for the economy as a whole. Firstly, by increasing the demand for investment while disincentivising savings, such a monetary policy is leading inexorably to inflationary pressures, as a greater proportion of investment is financed by credit expansion, and less is covered by households, businesses or indeed the government restraining their consumption. The net result is that Britain has some of the lowest levels of saving *and* investment among developed economies; in fact, our private investment as a proportion of the economy has been consistently lower in Britain than in any other G7 economy.

And secondly, by reducing the premium on risk, easy money reduces the overall *quality* of investment, as more capital makes its way towards ventures that would not receive financing under conditions in which risk was priced appropriately. This spreads new risks throughout the financial system, as well as explaining the persistence of failing 'zombie companies' who, but for cheap borrowing, would have been displaced by competition in the market. Some commentators have argued that zombie companies themselves create risks for the financial system, that concerns over systemic frailties further encouraged lower rates, and that this has discouraged both structural reforms to improve the competitiveness of the economy and new lending to more efficient firms – an instance of bad money chasing out good.[16]

Consumptionism thus distorts the investment process. And we see the impacts of this in our current account position. With low domestic savings, Britain increasingly must rely on overseas sources to fund its investment. And with low overall investment in the productive capacity of the economy, we are also failing to produce sufficient export goods and services with which to 'pay' for the imported goods we consume.

Trade imbalances might not be bad in and of themselves. But a chronic current account deficit like the one possessed by Britain reveals a basic inability to generate sufficient finance for investment, an economy that systematically privileges consumption over production, and a dependency on the import of foreign savings. Mark Carney once called this a reliance on the 'kindness of strangers'. But it is not a disinterested kindness; those foreign savings are being invested speculatively in a real estate market, for example, where demand vastly outstrips supply.[17]

Finally, consumptionism has serious fiscal implications too. Through taxation we generate the revenues required to fund our public services. Yet while our demand for a bigger state is rising – both because of an expanding population and because we are asking government to do more with its resources – our willingness to reduce private consumption to pay for it is not commensurate. And so instead of adjusting our expectations, we pass on the cost of funding our current demand for state services onto future generations in the form of debt.

The national debt is usually calculated to be about £2.5 trillion, or roughly 100 per cent of GDP. But the state of indebtedness in the UK is actually much more acute. Some of the most significant liabilities concern the state pension and public sector pension schemes. These schemes are not based upon the exercise of thrift and the setting aside of capital for tomorrow. Rather, the pension payments of today are being paid out of current revenues. And responsibility for funding the expected pension payments of those presently in work falls on the earnings of future generations. If one takes into account the forecasts for these liabilities, national debt stands at something closer to £11 trillion.[18]

This is the definition of short-termism, and the trade-off which higher debt implies between present consumption and future prosperity can be seen in more concrete fiscal terms too; debt interest payments, for example, currently exceed the amount of public money we spend in the UK on educating our children. It is sometimes argued that the sustainability of debt – the ability to service that debt year on year – is of greater importance to the public finances than the stock of total debt. But the latter is intimately bound up with the former, and in the long run, higher levels of debt will be inflationary, diminishing purchasing power and living standards in the future for the sake of borrowing today.

Inflation – of both the investment and fiscal variety – represents the monetary instantiation of economic irresponsibility and disownership. It facilitates the deferring of tough decisions about scarcity and the mismatch between the supply of goods and services and our demand for them, and it places the financial burden of that deferral upon future generations who have no capacity to voice their opposition. It is the means through which consumption today can be sustained and expanded by taking from the future. And it erodes the idea that obligations are owed from the present generation to the next.

A Political Economy of Short-Termism

Consumptionism involves an intergenerational transfer of resources – a tax on future prosperity to finance present expenditure. It is supported by a monetary system that acts like a time machine – bringing future resources into the present through debt, yet failing to generate sufficient improvements in our economic performance to service it.

But it also involves the *intra*generational transfer of resources via redistribution. Through progressive taxation, the economic technician can shift spending power from people with a low 'marginal propensity to consume' to demographics with a higher propensity. In so doing, they maximise 'aggregate demand' and increase the efficiency of consumption. The presumption is that those with high savings, assets or salaried earnings will not spend a maximally efficient amount of their income from the perspective of the overall efficiency of the economy, and that by redistributing some proportion of those resources towards others who might wish to spend more than they currently do, demand in the economy can be increased, thus supporting economic expansion.

If the object in question is to maximise total consumption, then the level of redistribution is never a question of principle, but only of degree. Some might argue that *all* forms of state-funded provision involve shifting wealth from one group to another – even those that do not aim at more efficient spending. But while the government is certainly engaging in 'redistribution' to improve the 'consumption' of the poorest in society when it offers a basic level of welfare to support the needy, it seems somehow misleading to label this as an exercise in consumption redistribution, rather than a society's collective commitment to provide a safety net below which no one should be able to fall into destitution. Surely this exercise must be distinguished as something altogether different from one which looks to increase the consumption of those lower on the income distribution in order to achieve some maximally efficient distribution of purchasing power.

Aside from the welfare system, the government can also indirectly seek to redistribute spending power through minimum wage provisions. While this may result in higher involuntary unemployment, it will boost the spending power of those in the lowest income groups (at least nominally), and those out of work might be compensated through the benefit system. For the consumptionist, this may still lead to higher overall consumer spending.

Consumptionism thus turns the economy into a 'vast revenue pumping station'. And treating the question of redistribution not as one of limited principle – that some minimum provision should be provided for the poorest by the well off and able – but as one of degree – that we should move spending power compulsorily to whoever has the highest marginal propensity to consume – means we have got into a situation where the *majority* of people are beneficiaries of state largesse, rather than contributors. In such a situation, spending power is being sloshed around back and forth between practically everyone in an attempt to engineer higher levels of consumption.[19]

For as long as the state relies on higher taxation to achieve this redistribution of spending power, the technician is promoting his ends using the resources of the present generation to maximise consumption. Once, however, it turns to deficit spending to increase the nominal incomes of those at the lower end of the earnings scale, it is sustaining present consumption through borrowing and thus shifting the financial burden onto the future. The distinction, though, is not exact. For higher rates of taxation to finance redistribution in the here and now impair the incentives to save in the present, and thus reduce the resources which are made available to augment future prosperity.

Regardless, the redistribution of spending power is another mode by which consumptionism attenuates the idea that prosperity is a partnership in which everyone has a personal stake. It not only hampers the instinct to set aside and to restrain – which is the true source of capital accumulation and improving living standards – but it also gives rise to the notion that it is the state and economic technicians who will engineer growth in the economy. If industry and the fruits of industry are subject to a higher rate of taxation while the government increasingly intervenes to guarantee a particular level of consumption, the incentives to simply enjoy a living standard secured by the state are heightened. Such a sentiment is highly destructive of the personal energy and assertiveness needed to sustain economic activity.

Human Quantitative Easing

The other essential component of the consumptionist agenda is unprecedentedly high levels of immigration. Of course, there is a version of immigration policy that should be considered a form of *investment*. It involves the welcoming of those with badly needed skills to this country, who want to develop a keen sense of stake in our economy, and who will increase the health and prosperity of our society. It involves, too, a considered attempt by government and society to integrate such people, to treat them with dignity as individuals, and to help furnish them with the cultural resources required to be contributing members of the wider community. A good deal of contemporary immigration is of precisely that nature.

But in recent years, an even greater proportion of our total net immigration has *not* been of that nature. Its principal justification, rather, has been to support the ends of consumptionism. By vastly expanding the supply of low-skilled human capital available to businesses operating in our country, mass immigration has partly been deployed as a device to keep labour costs low, goods and services affordable, and consumption high. The government itself benefits from this too; by importing more people to work in our health and social care sectors, for example, it can keep the show on the road without having to raise taxes or borrow more to address higher demand.

As many studies testify, however, mass immigration has simultaneously reduced the incentives for the public and private sector to invest the capital required to make our economy and public services more productive.[20] Indeed, the Migratory Advisory Committee has made precisely this assessment of the economic effects of Freedom of Movement since 2000, which it says has 'dampened incentives' to investment in plant and machinery that would augment productivity.[21]

Because of this, mass immigration has led to a 'dilution' of Britain's capital stock, as our infrastructure, plant, equipment, machinery and so on – investment in which remains subdued – is divided increasingly by a larger number of people. As such, though we observe that immigration boosts the overall size of the economy by increasing the number of people participating in it, the amount of economic output *per person* is stagnating partly as a consequence of these trends, because they increase the number of people in low-skilled employment while simultaneously discouraging steps that would grow the capital stock and improve productivity in those particular sectors of the economy.[22]

Furthermore, this mass immigration model has had a parasitical effect upon those institutions intimately connected to the future prosperity of our country, especially post-secondary school education. The business models of our universities have become dependent for their bottom line on continually expanding the number of foreign students – particularly those taking postgraduate qualifications – who pay higher fees. But while this might be profitable for the universities themselves, it has negative implications for the British economy.

On the one hand, universities are financially incentivised to cater to this market, and this has a crowding out effect on the resources available for training in skills that are in short supply within our domestic labour force. At the same time, many on graduate visas are coming to study courses of uncertain quality, bringing dependants and working in low-skilled sectors of the economy, which is contributing to the difficulties in raising productivity.

On the other hand, many of the university places in areas that will be vital to our future capacity to innovate – particularly in STEM subjects – are occupied by overseas students the majority of whom will return to their home countries.[23] In aggregate, the relationship between mass immigration and the university sector feeds our consumptionist model. It diverts attention and capital away from investment in the potential of younger people in Britain, actively discourages steps that would enhance the performance of many low productivity sectors of the economy, and entails that, in certain instances, we train the future labour forces of other countries at the expense of our own.

Mass immigration is a form of 'human quantitative easing', which like its monetary equivalent obviates the need to make the tough decisions in both the public and private sector required to increase our productivity and improve the living standards of future generations.[24] It is an important enabler of economic short-termism, and a key pillar of the consumptionist model.

The Structural Consequences of Consumptionism

The structural implications of consumptionism for the economy are significant. Firstly, consumptionism is a key driver in the expanding role of the state. In a context where risk is amplified and savings impaired, the demand for the state to intervene and to regulate investment is also increased. Eventually, the responsibility for investing in future prosperity is transposed onto the state itself. It can do this by 'derisking' certain types of investment and directing the private market to allocate capital into certain asset types or sectors, or alternatively, it can directly invest on our behalf by selling debt and increasing its own capital spending. But as the state competes with the private sector for limited capital, its efforts to promote public investment may well have a crowding out effect on business investment by increasing the cost of borrowing. At some point, it may therefore opt to 'force' a higher level of savings to finance investment by increasing taxes.

The present Labour government's economic programme is an experiment in precisely this approach to investment. It has identified that low investment is a key factor in Britain's lethargic productivity growth. Its proposed remedy, however, is not to improve the conditions that would lead to capital formation, but to assume this responsibility itself. It has started by simply increasing public sector borrowing and 'derisking' certain types of investment – particularly in green or renewable energy. But this has already had a negative impact on UK business investment, and before long is likely to necessitate even higher taxes.

In a context of lower investment and thus lower productivity, consumptionism also promotes a larger role for the state in labour markets. If prices are rising because of inflation but wages are not increasing from real improvements in production, consumption can be maintained by raising the nominal incomes of those on low earnings either through the minimum wage or through increasing the money supply. Ironically, these pressures have been intensified by a policy of mass immigration. In an attempt to keep costs for businesses low, vastly increasing the supply of labour has discouraged those steps in both the public and private sector that would improve productivity and *real* wages, and in so doing has made government intervention to arbitrarily inflate earnings even more popular.

Equally perceptible are the effects of consumptionism upon the moral and political psychology of those participating in the economy. The other side of the coin to an expanded remit for the state, after all, is a shrinking sphere for personal responsibility. Because it reduces the reward conferred for deferring consumption, stimulates inflation and pushes up taxes in order to redistribute spending power, consumptionism is highly productive of an anti-savings culture. And without savings, a person's provision for their own future is diminished, while their sense of responsibility for future prosperity is also inevitably impaired as well. Their willingness to outsource responsibility for both those tasks is correspondingly raised – and the idea that the state can itself furnish security and prosperity in equal measure gains currency. Consumptionism, in other words, is destructive of that sense of ownership which is the moral prerequisite of a free and prosperous economy.

Relatedly, consumptionism in practice also makes it harder for those in work to acquire a tangible stake in the economy in the form of property. Savings are the precondition for a wide distribution of private ownership. Higher taxation reduces the amount of income available for personal savings, while loose monetary policy has led to asset price inflation, which increases the height of the hurdle that an individual or household must surmount to acquire capital or purchase a home. Mass immigration in particular has exacerbated this situation dramatically by putting upward pressure on demand, particularly in London.[25] Consumptionism and the property-owning democracy are thus in a sense diametrically opposed political economies; one aims at the irresponsible satisfaction of present wants, the other is an undertaking to increase the number of people with a sense of responsibility in the long-term prosperity of their society.

At its core, consumptionism is yet another instantiation of the liberal rationalist approach to the economy. It treats it as an autonomous entity best managed by technicians, and it considers the individuals that participate within it as a means to the end of the economic machine. As such, it has the same, depersonalising, demoralising effects on the individual, transforming them from a complex moral being into a one-dimensional consumer.

In particular, by prioritising the ability to consume goods today, consumptionism ends up reducing the level of investment in people's ability to produce things of value or to learn new skills, as well as in the infrastructure that will enable them to lead lives of meaning and purpose. And this is just as true of the people who are coming to the UK, who instead of being invested in as valuable members of our wider community are treated simply as means to the end of sustaining our present levels of consumption. They are seen not as human persons but 'human capital' who in aggregate will help to keep labour costs low.

There is an intimate connection between our present approach to consumption, savings and investment and our deteriorating manufacturing capacity, our low productivity and the disastrous job market that young adults are entering, which comprises a mixture of poorly paid and precarious work and exorbitantly well-paid jobs in a financial services sector which in some instances operates to inflate the values of existing assets rather than assist capital towards those parts of the economy that will promote future prosperity – a sector, as the economist Roger Bootle has put it, often incentivised to promote 'distributive' rather than 'creative' gains.

A system which sustains aggregate demand but leaves people with forms of employment that are low skilled and which present limited opportunities for advancement and the building up of capital are unconducive to human flourishing and must be counted as one of the key features of our broader economic malaise.

Our persistent current account deficits, high levels of indebtedness, and our chronically low levels of saving and investment are thus not really technical problems best solved by some directing agency, but the symptoms of a moral transformation in society that has seen decision-making responsibility flow from the personal domain towards the state, and has rendered individuals far less future-regarding.

In asking government to take on a greater role in satisfying our present wants and needs, consumptionism weakens certain vital instincts. If the state will guarantee you a particular level of consumption, why thrift and save – especially when those savings will either be limited by taxation or eroded in value by inflation? Why support those in your community on a voluntary basis if the state will simply force you to do so? Why fret about the inheritance being passed on to future generations if debts can simply be inflated away or bounced on indefinitely?

Alongside this moral transformation of the individual from complex moral being to mere consumer, it is also worth mentioning the role that the decline of the family in our culture has had in the shift away from the bourgeois and towards the consumptionist economic paradigm. For it is primarily out of a concern for the family unit that the future-orientated tendency in human nature has manifested itself.[26] Familial solidarity is the thing that extends a person's identity through time, and which connects them with the past and future in an intimate way. The desire to provide for a partner or offspring or to pass on something of value spurs the willingness to restrain present consumption.

But as fewer people get married and have children, as family is reconceptualised as a burden or encumbrance which people ought to be liberated from, and with the very notion of passing on an inheritance increasingly contested on ethical grounds, so the individual as consumer is less willing to assume the responsibility they previously undertook to work hard, save and invest in order to provide for future generations.

Economic Responsibility, Savings and Investment

In many ways, Modern Monetary Theory represents the consumptionist case taken to its logical extremity. It considers the state to have an infinite capacity to sustain consumption through issuing currency. 'Instead of arguing over the monetary cost' of government programmes, argues Stephanie Kelton, politicians should be thinking about how government can best meet 'the needs of our entire population' by 'taking over the economic steering wheel'. It sees taxes not as the means by which to fund public services but to engineer the 'distribution of wealth and income', increase consumption, and 'encourage or discourage certain behaviours' – in sum, to *use* people to improve economic performance.[27]

By running deficits, modern monetary theorists argue that the state should take away debt from the private economy and assume that debt itself. They reject the idea that we are as individuals and households in any way 'personally liable for some portion of the national debt', and argue that by, calling for an expansion of public debt, they are advocating for '*more* fiscal responsibility . . . not less. We just need to redefine what it means to budget our resources responsibly.'[28]

Such prescriptions are the very opposite of economic responsibility. The consumptionist logic behind them saps at the values of ownership which sustains our shared prosperity. It tears at people's sense of intergenerational obligation, and treats individuals as consumers who are but means to the end of maximising overall consumption. The effects of this on the human character have in turn subdued the motivation to be self-sufficient, the willingness to make sacrifices in the cause of widening and deepening prosperity, and the overall vitality of the economy.

Retrieving this situation and restoring the economy to health will require an approach orientated around an understanding that humans are more than mere consumers, one that is committed to the idea that prosperity is an intergenerational partnership which bestows obligations upon those who are living towards those who are yet to be born. It will require us, in other words, to abandon consumptionism, not to double down on it as modern monetary theorists suggest.

In the first instance, this means the renewal of a culture that respects savings. Of course, it is not straightforwardly the case that saving is virtuous and consumption is licentious. The situation is much more complex. Higher savings inevitably implies lower consumption for some groups in society. Moreover, as stated, the ultimate purpose of savings itself is to provide for some level of consumption in the future. Nevertheless, if we are to build a high productivity economy of decent skilled employment and improved prospects for future generations, this will necessarily involve us addressing our pitifully low savings rate. For in the long run, it is savings that will determine the level of real investment in the productive capacity of the economy.

The question, of course, is whose consumption will be restrained in order to facilitate a higher level of savings? The answer must be the state's, as its expenditure now consumes almost half the economy, leaving fewer resources for productive sectors. Some may well argue that reducing public consumption would be to reduce the 'social wage' or the sum of benefits and services that people receive, including those provided by the state. But the quality of this social wage being offered to the public at present is pitiful and represents exceptionally poor value for taxpayer money. So the object ought to be to cut the state's consumption to then boost personal and household savings.

The cumulative effects of liberal rationalism and consumptionist policies have badly damaged the instincts to thrift and save, though. Thus, it will not be sufficient simply to cut government consumption in order to promote greater savings. The state has quite energetically diminished the propensity to save in Britain through taxation, loose monetary policy and redistribution. Now, equally energetic efforts are required to reverse that damage.

It is time to restore the idea that our collective prosperity is a multigenerational partnership in which we all have a stake; that the economy is not some distant dispensing machine for meeting our consumption demands in the present, but an enterprise for which we all need to take personal ownership if it is to succeed. We can no longer afford to use up the vital sources of our long-term capacity to flourish simply to meet present wants and desires. Indeed, it is our responsibility now to replenish them.

5

Welfare, Healthcare and Social Care

It is all too often forgotten that anyone who is serious about human dignity should measure progress less by what the state does for the masses than by the degree to which the masses themselves solve the problem of their rainy day out of their own resources and on their own responsibility. This, and only this, is worthy of free and grown-up persons.[1] – Wilhelm Röpke

In a totalitarian society all action outside the citizens' home . . . is directed or controlled by the state. By contrast, vigour and abundance of voluntary action outside one's home, individually and in association with other citizens, for bettering one's own life and that of one's fellows, are the distinguishing marks of a free society.[2] – William Beveridge

Compulsion versus Compassion

Patriotic Millionaires is a curious charity. Established in 2021, they describe themselves as 'a network of British millionaires' campaigning for higher levels of taxation on the wealthy, increased spending on the welfare state, and greater levels of redistribution through the tax system. Their stated object is to challenge the 'concentration of wealth and power', to promote greater wealth equality, and to 'build a more just, stable, and inclusive economy' in the UK. They argue that reducing taxes is a 'reckless risk' that 'will cost our country', and that the only route to greater household financial security – and indeed 'happiness' itself – is by taxing more.

What is so interesting about this organisation is that they are representative of a widely held understanding of the state, social provision and responsibility in our society. This is a charity with vast networked resources and wealth, yet who believe that their time and energy is better spent on campaigning for higher taxes and a larger state than on directly or voluntarily addressing the subjects they care about. Their view appears to be that *only* the state can secure the broader social ends they seek, and that implicitly the state is a better judge of how to use wealth than individual families or communities.

It is an increasingly prevalent understanding of the welfare state in contemporary British society. But it is one which fails to recognise that higher taxes and greater government social provision *itself* creates a much graver inequality between the state and the public, that the size of the state and the scope for individual moral action are *negatively* – not positively – correlated, and that ever greater state provision of our societal wants and needs necessarily damages the single most important resource we have for building a better society – that is, our capacity for generosity, and the propensity to take personal ownership for the trials and difficulties of others.

Any decent, civilised society will have systems of support and aid that protect all from the possibility of falling into abject poverty. These lifelines are not a subject of debate – they are an authentic communal expression of solidarity with the least fortunate in our country. The question, however, is how far that level of provision ought to go, and whether it might have harmful societal effects if carried too far.

The growing role of the state in social provision – and the inability of many to envisage or countenance a world in which non-state actors have a prominent part to play – is the political manifestation of our reduced readiness to shoulder the responsibility for the needy in our community, and of a willingness to outsource such responsibility to the state.

The consequences of that outsourcing for the economy are dire – it makes us all less independent and self-sufficient, it destroys incentives, it makes it harder to generate the revenues that fund vital public services, and it has played a part in making the British people less engaged in the nation's socio-economic fortunes. But above all else, it has vitiated the belief that we ought to take personal ownership for ourselves and for others in need, which is itself a form of poverty.

Liberal Rationalism, Equality and the Welfare State

In any decent society, providing for the neediest is a moral obligation. The rich help the poor. People are not left in conditions which negate their inherent dignity as human beings in illness, old age or infirmity. Individuals are supported if they cannot work, and assisted when they are looking for work. And there is little reason to think that this level of provision ought not to rise as a society becomes more prosperous. But there are many methods by which that minimum sustenance and support might be provided; many means by which burdens might be shared across society between households, community and the government; and many ways in which families, voluntary organisations and indeed responsible individuals might ensure that level of provision without recourse to state compulsion.

Yet aside from some isolated attempts to present an alternative, there are effectively only two perspectives on the purpose of social policy offered today.[3] The first considers it to be an exercise in how best to deploy the power of the state to solve every challenge we face, and in so doing to relieve us of the inconvenience of addressing them ourselves. In this view, all our social challenges, including provision for the poor, the care of children and the elderly, and the securing of our personal healthiness, are technical in nature, and since the state is the most effective and powerful tool at the disposal of society, so it is also the most appropriate instrument for 'solving' these myriad challenges.

This viewpoint has defined the terms of the entire debate around public services in Britain. On the one side are those who believe we should raise taxes in order to increase expenditure on public services. On the other are those who are cautious about increasing taxes because of their distorting effects on economic incentives. But there is not a fundamental divergence in perspective in this debate over what the state ought to be for when it comes to social provision. Those cautioning against higher taxes generally make their case on the grounds of *efficiency*: that lower taxes will promote economic expansion, which will subsequently lead to greater resources for state services. They do not often accompany this with any form of moral case against the state performing certain activities. The debate around public service provision is one of *degree*, not *principle*.

The second perspective with considerable currency in this country is that the purpose of social policy and state welfare is to promote greater wealth equality throughout society. It moves from the decent and incontestable view that the surpluses of some should be sacrificed for the urgent need of others to the presumption that an inequality of means in society is inherently bad, and that social policy should aim at the near equalisation of people's material conditions.[4] Since public services are funded through a progressive system of taxation, government expenditure is a means by which purchasing power is transferred from one group in society to another, and thus also a means of advancing equality. By raising taxes or making them more progressive, that transfer can be extended or intensified.

Sometimes the economic case is made that this distributes demand more efficiently. Other times the case is made that greater wealth equality is good in and of itself. But the end sought is usually the same. And again, within the political debate, opponents of this perspective do not usually argue against the principle of seeking greater wealth equality, but against the degree to which efforts to promote equality might impair economic incentives for work and enterprise.

Fundamentally, these two perspectives are unified by the view that the state is the principal actor in social policy, and that state provision is wholly preferable to non-state provision. They are presented as idealistic views of mankind, yet in reality, they are deeply *misanthropic* ones, for implicitly they assume that individuals cannot be genuinely altruistic themselves, but must be forced to be so through the state.[5] And without a countervailing viewpoint, these two perspectives in combination have had a ratcheting effect on the size and scope of government welfare in this country.

Over time, state provision has got wider and deeper. It now supports a far greater number of people with a growing range of issues, from those incapable of working due to long-term mental health problems through to relatively well-off pensioners with the cost of their energy bills. At any one time, the Department for Work and Pensions is making payments to over 20 million people, or around *a third* of the British population.

In the context of an ageing population, the British state is committed to spending a perpetually rising amount on the state pension, and to meeting almost all people's health costs from cradle to grave. We spend roughly £320 billion per annum on social protection including the state pension, and about £200 billion on health – together roughly half a trillion pounds, almost half annual government expenditure, and about 20 per cent of the entire UK economy. The increasing size of the state is being driven largely by growing expenditure on welfare and healthcare (in addition to the rising cost of debt discussed earlier), and the size of the state as a proportion of the economy has increased from around 35 per cent in the 1990s to over 45 per cent today.

The welfare state ceased to be primarily a vehicle for supporting the weakest and most needy long ago, and now acts instead as a comprehensive provider of services for vast swathes of the population. That is in keeping with dominant understandings of the purpose of the welfare state: that its task is either to address each and all our social provision requirements, or to redistribute spending power more equally and efficiently throughout society. Theoretically, these perspectives place no limits on the state's involvement in social provision, or its level of expenditure.

Perhaps the clearest evidence for this is the proportion of people who are net recipients of state welfare. Some 54 per cent of people now receive more in benefits than they contribute through the tax system.[6] Structurally, welfare spending does not reflect a commitment on the part of the strong to help the weak anymore; it represents the state's increasing pervasiveness in people's lives, as it moves spending power from one person to another and goes about relieving as many people as possible of the burden of providing for themselves.

The opponents of 'welfarism' – that is, an ideological commitment to an expansive state welfare – correctly highlight the immediate damage it does to incentives within the economy. Jon Moynihan has updated some earlier studies on the relationship between the size of the state as a proportion of GDP and annual growth rates, and found not only that they are negatively correlated, but that there is a causal relationship: 'all the evidence implies', he writes, 'that as government grows in size (as a proportion of the economy), growth slows and unemployment rises'.[7] Between 1960 and 2019, the average annual growth rate in countries where the size of the state amounted to 25–30 per cent of the economy was fully two and a half percentage points higher than countries where it consumed 40–50 per cent.

Yet the harmful effects of welfarism run much deeper. Of course, a state that confiscates more of the pound that people earn to fund its spending deprives the latter of the fruits of their labour, dimming their enterprise and industry. And it is true that this will in turn inhibit the very source of the revenues that pay for our public services. But the level of taxation and spending in our economy is in principle transient; it can be modified by a government with sufficient political will.

Of far greater concern is that successive governments have proven entirely unwilling to do just this. And this reflects the much more deep-seated damage that welfarism has wrought on our society. Politicians by and large reflect their electorates, and the British electorate has become eager to see responsibility for social provision taken out of their hands and given to the state. The expansion of state welfare has decayed that instinct to take personal responsibility for oneself and for those in the community.

Robbing Peter to Pay Paul

If the liberal rationalist consensus on welfare was correct, we should have become more adept at addressing our many social challenges as our society has progressed technically and technologically. That we have not is a source of confusion for some, but it should not be. How we go about addressing the needs of the poorest or weakest or most vulnerable in society is an *ethical* question, not a technical one.[8] The moral consequences of our present system – in which able people are discouraged from taking personal ownership of their circumstances – are ruinous. Indeed in many ways, as our society has become more technologically advanced, more networked, more digital, the capacity of communities to address the ethical dilemma of social provision has waned.

Our ever-expanding welfare state greatly modifies the 'vertical' relationship between government and governed. The constant increase in the breadth and depth of state social provision is driven at least in part by the vague idea that when we empower the state, we are in some way empowering ourselves – that as the state grows more powerful, we are in some way rendered more free. But this is a false and dangerous idea. It stems from the same elision of power and freedom which enabled certain philosophers to argue mendaciously that one can be 'forced to be free'.[9] It involves a rejection of the idea that the individual person ought as far as possible to be responsible for the path they take through life. It permits the treatment of humans as means towards the ends of others, which is to reject the very basis of a politics based on personalism.

Welfarism also transforms the 'horizontal' relationships *between* people within society. When the call is made for an increase in state expenditure or a widening of the scope of state activities, there is often an assumption that the funding for this additional assistance is to be taken from some source of revenue external to the public, or from a particular group of rich people who can be squeezed further, or that we can simply borrow the money to pay for such services without any immediate pain or burden. Yet such calls are always a demand by some citizens upon fellow citizens. That burden cannot be expunged or permanently removed from the ledger of public liabilities, but must be paid for if not via taxation, then through inflation and decreased future living standards.

And ultimately, to generate sufficient revenues to support the modern state, squeezing the very rich will always be insufficient. The top 10 per cent of earners already account for some 35 per cent of all tax income. These are mobile people, many of whom are opting to leave the UK and pay their taxes elsewhere. And so, the burden must inevitably fall upon the middle earners. Peter must be paid out of the savings of Paul. The relationship between citizens becomes instrumental; other people become the means by which my own needs and wants might be satisfied. And the state lives up to its reputation as that great fiction 'by which everyone seeks to live at the expense of everyone else'.[10]

All of this erodes the vital impulse to provide for oneself against the vicissitudes of the human condition. But it does something else too. It shifts the centre of gravity for moral decision-making further away from the personal and local and towards the collective, and shrinks the space in which individuals can exercise responsibility and moral agency.

To its advocates, statism is coterminous with generosity. The more we pay in taxes and the more we spend on social provision, the more giving, the more compassionate, the more *humane* we are. But this is a misleading conflation. State provision is *compulsory* provision, and an expanding welfare state correspondingly deprives people of their ability to freely offer 'the gift of self', which is the basis of all morality. A society whose structures and institutions make it harder for its citizens to give this gift of self is also diminishing their capacity for flourishing.[11]

Welfare

Liberal rationalism is built deep into the operating logic of Britain's welfare state, which seems deliberately designed to absolve people of responsibility. Take our approach to mental health benefits, where the current system – though well-intentioned – traps many people in dependency and passivity, rather than helping them reclaim control over their lives. The explosion of caseloads for a selection of disability and incapacity benefits (or so-called health-related benefits) over the last half decade since the pandemic has been unprecedented. In fact, it is barely believable. As the Institute for Fiscal Studies found recently:

> Total health-related benefits spending for all ages has increased from £52 billion in 2019–20 to £65 billion in 2023–24. The increase in working-age spending has been mostly driven by an increasing caseload: from 2.2 million in 2019–20 to 3.2 million

> in 2023–24 for disability benefits (39% growth) and from 2.5 million in 2019–20 to 3.2 million in 2023–24 for incapacity benefits (28% growth).[12]

Policy Exchange has forecast that the total cost of health-related benefits to the taxpayer will rise to £100 billion by 2030.[13] And most of this growth in caseloads and costs has been driven by new claimants with mental health–related issues, not higher awards. Take Personal Independence Payments (PIP), the main disability benefit. Since 2019–20, awards granted for those with mental health–related issues like anxiety or depression have increased by 190 per cent.[14] Claimants with learning, social or behavioural issues have increased fourfold, but make up a far smaller proportion of the overall case load than awards for mental health issues.

Once people are on these forms of support, they tend to remain on them. Some two-thirds of new PIP claimants are still receiving it, for example, five years on. Many rely on these payments to help with the cost of living with a disability. But significant numbers receive PIP for conditions which do not add to their cost of living, and which ought to be treated entirely differently if the object is to return people to a position of control in their lives. For these claimants, PIP is generating dependency, not independence.[15]

Many of these claimants will be in work and receiving support on a needs-tested basis. But others will be deemed out of work because of their disability – and a growing proportion of those people because of a mental health–related disability. There are now around 9.5 million people between the ages of 16 and 64 who are classed as economically inactive in the UK – 2.8 million of those are considered long-term sick. These people are not actively looking for work. They do not show up in the unemployment figures, and are largely condemned to dependency on state support and worklessness. And whereas about a third of unemployed people find work within six months, just 1 per cent of those who are economically inactive due to long-term sickness find employment in the same period.[16]

This is of course an economic issue. But far more importantly, it is a moral travesty, and a gross waste of human potential. In Grimsby and Birkenhead, over half the population is on out of work benefits.[17] We comfort ourselves that through our tax contributions, we have somehow taken responsibility for them. But these are ultimately people who have been forgotten about.

There is a large number of people who will need state support, often continuously throughout their lives. A decent system of social provision should recognise this. But that is not really in question. The real issue is the large number of people who are dependent on the state, but ought not to be, and who could live self-sufficient lives. State welfare is failing these people.

The number of people reporting a mental health condition has roughly doubled over the last decade. There is a debate to be had about whether this is a genuine increase in people with conditions, or whether changes in reporting are simply uncovering a problem that already existed. Regardless, the question is: what is the most humane response to people with such challenges; what support is most likely to enable them to flourish? Our present system offers cash support but does very little to give people control over their lives.

Much of our contemporary approach towards mental health in society – particularly among younger generations – has been defined by what Jonathan Haidt and Greg Lukianoff have termed 'safetyism', a form of concept creep in which the laudable end of promoting people's physical safety has transformed into a dogmatic quest to eliminate risk entirely from society. It is 'a culture or belief system in which safety has become a sacred value, which means that people become unwilling to make trade-offs demanded by other practical and moral concerns. '"Safety" trumps everything else, no matter how unlikely or trivial the potential danger.'[18]

Safetyism encourages us to shield people from the stresses and strains of life; to alleviate people from the responsibility of having to deal with those mental challenges which are ineliminable aspects of the human condition. It feels kind and compassionate when we assist people to extract themselves from their university courses or from the workplace to shield them from mental and emotional challenges. But it leaves each person it touches less well equipped to live well.

Healthcare

Healthcare is usually considered as a separate government function to welfare. But that is not how the founders of the modern welfare state understood it. The Beveridge Report, that founding document of the British welfare state, lamented that the many social services that had existed prior to the Second World War 'had been dealt with separately, with little or no reference to allied problems'. It proposed an integrated system of state provision, whereby the state could address the evils of want, disease, ignorance, squalor and idleness together. A 'comprehensive national health service' was a 'logical corollary' of such a system of state social provision.[19] And just as with other forms of welfare provision, our present healthcare system encourages people to relinquish ownership for their own situation and pass it up to the state.

The National Health Service (NHS) is a quintessentially liberal rationalist creation, or what Harry Eckstein called a victory for 'radical managerialism'.[20] It sought to replace an 'irrational' patchwork of different providers and traditional institutions with a centralised and standardised service. And it has acquired a quasi-religious status in British society. Thousands of excellent, public-spirited people work in its hospitals and agencies, and many receive good quality care through the service.

But the NHS's very design is preventing it from delivering the quality of healthcare that ought to be expected in a country like Britain. Its performance is at best middling when placed in international comparison, with some alarmingly poor outcomes on specific metrics like healthy life expectancy, where it is the second worst performer across countries with a similar level of economic development. It has a comparatively high rate of preventable and avoidable mortalities. Average waiting times from referral to treatment in England have also doubled since 2008.[21]

What is the structural issue with our healthcare system? By funding provision entirely through progressive taxation, socialised systems tend to weaken the connection between rights (the access to services) and responsibilities (bearing the costs associated with their use). Individuals consume healthcare that is free at the point of delivery, regardless of how much they contribute, and without facing any direct cost for additional use. Yet increasing taxes to fund rising demand creates economic distortions, disincentivising work and enterprise, and potentially weakening the revenue base needed to sustain the system. That is the core *economic* dilemma.

The deeper issue is moral, however. The NHS is perhaps the state institution in which liberal rationalist thinking has become most embedded. For many in the health policy establishment, the NHS is an end in itself, to which the lives of individuals should be modified and adapted. In a fully socialised model, individuals are largely insulated from the financial consequences of their health-related choices. But as responsibility for keeping healthy flows upwards towards the state, so must choice and decision-making power. Instead of asking people to take responsibility for their lifestyle and behaviour, the state bans activities. To a growing extent, the behaviour of individuals and groups of individuals must be adapted to safeguard our healthcare model.

We saw this, of course, during the pandemic, in which it was remarkably easy for the government to impose significant restrictions on people's private lives – even their ability to interact with family – in order to 'protect the NHS'. Perhaps the greatest evidence for how anti-personalist our present approach to healthcare has become, however, is to be found in the debate around assisted suicide. Empowering the state to offer end of life 'services', it has been argued, is key to the affordability of socialised healthcare in the context of an ageing population.[22] Human life itself is coming to be seen as a means to supporting a particular model of healthcare provision, as we begin to value people based on the cost of their care. We must not shy away from the fact that *in extremis*, this is what follows when responsibility and freedom flow upwards, away from the personal and towards the impersonal. State-assisted suicide is the logical terminus of the liberal rational mindset, in which people become expendable.

This is why we need an approach to healthcare provision that deliberately aims to push choice and responsibility back downwards. Of course, no one in the UK could seriously advocate for a purely private healthcare model, in which the state plays no role. The United States, for example, stands as a stark warning: a system that combines crippling unaffordability, limited coverage and often poorer outcomes. This model is worse than the one we presently have.

But the NHS, in its current form – where the funding, purchasing and provision of services are all entirely socialised – offers few incentives for individuals to maintain their own health or minimise the burden they place on others. Moreover, it has contributed to the erosion of non-state organisations that once played a meaningful role in social provision. Prior to the NHS, Britain had a flourishing network of voluntary hospitals, friendly societies and mutual aid institutions that supported health and care services within communities. Perhaps the state is required to deliver the minimum safety net expected of any legitimate government today. But it is certainly not the case that the best system of healthcare is one that is totally and wholly socialised.

The State Pension

The issue with our approach to pension provision ultimately relates to the same problem: it actively encourages people to absolve themselves of responsibility and cede it to the state.

Annual expenditure on pension-age benefits has grown by about 80 per cent since 2002.[23] This is largely due to two factors. Firstly, the UK's ageing population means that people are living – and thus receiving support from the state – for longer. Since the state pension was first introduced in 1908, life expectancy in the UK has almost doubled.[24] Yet the age at which people begin to receive their state pension has actually *fallen*, from 70 then to 66 today (and 67 from 2026).

Secondly, the 'triple lock' has ensured that since 2010, year on year the state pension has risen by the highest of inflation, wage growth or 2.5 per cent. As a result, spending on this benefit has risen from 3.8 per cent of annual GDP to over 5 per cent.[25] If one includes pension credit and winter fuel payments, it is closer to 6 per cent.

Many retirees believe that the state pension is an entitlement which they themselves have funded over their working lives. But that is not how our state pension works at all. Yes, a record of tax contributions is required to draw the state pension. There is not, however, a 'fund' which individuals pay into, which grows over time, and which bears interest. Instead, we have a 'pay as you go' system in which today's pensions are paid by those currently in work. This introduces a disconnect between the act of working, earning and saving, and the provision for people in retirement, which in turn politicises the system of provision for old age. The triple-locked state pension, is, in other words, a system of escalating obligations for future generations, divorced from any shared ethic of responsibility.

Government spending on the state pension is presently just over £130 billion per annum. The IFS estimates that, if unreformed, it will cost anywhere between £5 and £40 billion extra each year by 2050 than if pensions simply rose in line with average earnings. There is thus a further disconnect between the social provision for pensioners and the earnings of those who pay for it through taxes each year, since the scale of spending on the state pension increases, regardless of whether the means for funding it improves. This is a system of fiscal *irresponsibility* – and must either be funded through higher taxes or, more likely, by passing off the burden to future generations in the form of debt.

Social Care

Liberal rationalism finds it easy to justify writing a blank cheque for pensions. But it has an inherent difficulty dealing with those in need of care in old age. Because they lack an economic 'function', it has a challenge in establishing precisely how they ought to be treated. For some, it is simply a matter of providing for their immediate physical care needs as cheaply as possible, with little broader consideration of what goes into a life of meaning. Which is why care provision is limited, care workers are undervalued and paid very little, and social care is somewhat swept under the political carpet – passed by Westminster onto local authorities which are struggling to meet their statutory responsibilities to deliver care. It is why government after government has opted to kick the can of social care reform further down the road – 'out of sight, out of mind, and out of pocket', as Danny Kruger has put it.[26]

As it stands, social care is paid for by local authorities on a statutory basis, funded by council tax and central government grants (service provision itself, for both residential care homes and at home care, is overwhelmingly private). Total government spending on social care is some £27 billion a year and supports about 900,000 people, roughly 550,000 of which are elderly individuals either receiving at-home care or living in a care home; millions more have private assistance or rely on unpaid support, often from family.[27] There is a tight means test for accessing state social care; those with assets over the upper limit of £23,250 are ineligible for support; only those with assets below £14,240 are not charged for the cost of their care.

The value of one's home is included in that asset calculation, except if another family member continues to live in that home. Yet given that the majority will stay at home if they have a spouse or partner, most people attempting to access funded residential care will have their home included in their asset calculation. Only about one in ten people are thus eligible for support, and the government believes that one in seven over 65s will face care costs of over £100,000.[28]

Social care is certainly a financial issue. The main funding stream is council tax, but increases in council tax are already limited by statute and are deeply unpopular. Meeting extra social care demand therefore often comes at the expense of local authority spending on other core areas, like bin collection, highway maintenance, libraries and so on. The limited resource available is partly why the means test is so stringent.

But the problems surrounding the provision of social care are not merely pecuniary. Social care ought to be about giving people a sense of purpose and agency in later life – about their roles not first and foremost as economic actors but as parents and grandparents, and elders in communities. A decent social care policy should be concerned with 'giving people a life', not just meeting their immediate physical needs.[29] The present system fails to do this.

Some have argued that the solution to this situation is to have a fully tax-funded system akin to the NHS with universal coverage and a cap on lifetime care costs. This is a totally misguided approach. We need to counter the tendency to pass off responsibility for the care of the elderly to some impersonal state, and push ownership for care back down towards the local community, and most importantly, the family. The starting point of a new approach to care must be an effort to situate the elderly within a web of close and personal relationships, where they can find a warmth and intimacy which a socialised and centralised system would never be able to provide.

An Alternative Vision

One of the most dangerous ideas about welfarism and ever-growing government expenditure on social provision is that these trends are inevitable. That personal responsibility and voluntary provision are essentially outdated in the complex and integrated world we inhabit today, and that only government has the capacity for the coordinated action required to deliver mass assistance in welfare and healthcare.

But the version of welfarism which defines policymaking today is a departure from the vision of social provision advanced even by the principal founders of the welfare state. William Beveridge, its chief architect in Britain, did not believe in the inexorability of an omnicompetent state with an ever-expanding remit of responsibilities. On the contrary, he saw such omnicompetence to be the hallmark of an unfree society, and voluntary provision either by families or by individuals in association with one another as 'the distinguishing marks of a free society'.[30] The issue is not whether or not there should be tax-funded welfare provision. Of course there should be. It is whether the state should be the only, or even the principal form of welfare provision, or if it should be part of a much more pluralistic system.

It is certainly difficult politically to reverse the growth of an excessively large welfare state. Depriving people of actual and tangible benefits or services in the here and now on the promise of a better life in the future is a course of action fraught with danger in a democracy. Each incremental increase in the size of the state is tempting for the politician to offer, and gratifying for those in receipt of its largesse. But each effort to pare back the state is painful in an obvious and identifiable way. Committing to indefinite rises in the amount paid in pension benefits is easy; reducing the liberality of pension payments is far harder.

A more fundamental issue, however, is that attempts to shrink the role of the state in society are invariably seen as cruel or unkind towards the needy. Which is why advocates of a smaller state couch their arguments in the language of efficiency, while conceding the moral terrain to those who equate statism with compassion.

And so those in favour of efforts to reduce welfarism are only ever seen as offering a more frugal version of the liberal rationalist conception of social provision, in which the only limit on the state's activities is that set by how much revenue it can extract from the public. They are hampered, in other words, by the absence of a compelling, alternative vision of social provision to the statist model; a moral vision, connected to a higher order of values about the good life, about responsibility, and about obligation; a vision which dismantles the erroneous conflation of a bigger state with greater compassion or generosity.

This situation, in which in the absence of any alternative form of provision an expansionary state fills the void, is the legacy of liberal rationalism. Not only is it responsible for the progressive diminution of those forms of community and civil association which used to perform vital social functions throughout society; it has also inhibited people's ability to imagine that those functions could now be performed by anything *other* than the state. Which is why organisations like Patriotic Millionaires with whom we started this chapter campaign for higher taxes, rather than seeking to direct their capital towards innovative ways of meeting the demand for social support.

What, then, is the basis for a new, alternative vision? Firstly, it must reject the view that the purpose of social provision is the equalisation of wealth, either as a good in itself, or in the cause of a more efficient distribution of spending power. For such a view is entirely incompatible with a politics committed to the treatment of individuals as ends in themselves. To make everyone materially equal, one must inevitably treat people unequally – as means to achieving some plan for the aggregate.

Instead, it must be a personalist approach to social provision – one committed to expanding the opportunities for people to take ownership for their own lives, and resisting the enlargement of the state which constricts those opportunities. This is in many ways its own commitment to equality – the equal dignity of all human beings as inherently valuable.

Similarly, it must be one which rejects the view that all issues of social provision are technical challenges which can best be overcome by centralised administration. Rather, it must embrace the idea of subsidiarity: that the state should concern itself with a limited number of activities which only it is capable of performing; that it should avoid as far as possible intervening in lower levels of community and social existence, for in doing so, it may deprive society of those energies essential to its strength and vigour.

And thirdly, it must not commit the failing of other recent governments which have sought to shrink the state but not produced a credible plan for what will replace it in areas of social provision. In a context in which the bonds of responsibility and personal ownership have been badly severed, a proactive effort must be made to restore the communities and associations which are the basis of self-sufficient people – families, neighbourhoods, churches and voluntary organisations. Otherwise, the withdrawal of the state will extend the individualisation and atomisation which promoted increased state dependency in the first place.

The choice to be made is not between a compassionate yet profligate social policy of expanding state welfare, and a crueller yet more fiscally responsible version of the same thing. It is between two quite divergent understandings of compassion and of how best to enable people to flourish – between one in which the state relieves people of the need to care for themselves and for one another, and one in which it is understood that humans flourish when they are situated in genuine communities in which they can take ownership of their own lives and share in the responsibility of providing for the needy.

Nor should those who wish to reduce the degree to which the state compulsorily provides for people confuse their own case with a denial of the genuine need for structures of support in our society. The case to be made, rather, is that in many instances those structures of support would be better delivered through proximate forms of association at a human scale, rather than the cold and impersonal agencies of the state.

The moral thread running through all these points is that of personal ownership – a humane and compassionate approach to social provision must be dedicated to widening, not shrinking the opportunities for people to have ownership over their own lives, and for people to be personally responsible for others. Our statist approach to social provision, which considers the state a provider of first resort rather than a safety net, fails to do this.

Poverty as Disownership

Any system of social provision should be designed to provide a degree of security in people's lives against the fluctuations and uncertainties of the human condition. But security can be a slippery concept, and certain definitions of security themselves can be used as pretext for further statism. Those in favour of a larger state identify the very real sense of insecurity born out of the decay of civil society and an economy which offers too few prospects for the accumulation of capital, and contend that this is the justification for an expanded, more active role for the state in guaranteeing people's security.

But the security they aim at is of a particular relative income and standard of living determined in comparison with that of others – one which can only be secured by state intervention and redistribution through taxes.[31] Such an approach reduces the opportunities for households to provide for their own security; high minimum wages and tighter labour market regulations lead to job losses, and higher taxes makes it harder for those of average means to generate the savings necessary for their own provision. This increasingly makes security a gift bestowed by the state, rather than something that can be earned and achieved independently.

A level of security, though, a 'minimum standard of life and labour below which a man or a woman of goodwill, however old and weak, will not be able to fall', is the prerequisite of any good society.[32] The purpose of social policy ought to be the reduction of *absolute* poverty – the sort of indigence that robs individuals of their dignity and leaves them unable to flourish. This would be an approach that better reflected the organic and shared sense of obligation between humans in a particular community, rather than some particular plan for living standards or wealth distribution to which people are to be bent and directed.

Just as important, however, is *how* one proposes to eliminate poverty. For many, poverty is simply a matter of material living standards, which can be addressed through money transfers from the well off to the needy via the state. But poverty is not simply a pecuniary condition, or a shortage of money. As a 'human condition' rather than merely a 'statistical condition', poverty is defined just as much by how one meets their human needs – whether they are absolutely dependent on strangers for their sustenance and support, or whether they have the resources of friends or family or a community to fall back on.

Poverty from this perspective means to have lost a sense of stake in one's future, to have lost *ownership* over one's fortunes. And it is entirely plausible that proposed remedies that increase the cash at disposal of people in need in the immediate term might in fact have demoralising consequences, increasing their dependency, and reducing their prospects of gaining control of their lives.[33] A policy of simply paying people to achieve a minimum living standard, or one that leaves people dependent on the state, is a form of palliative care, rather than a genuine solution to impoverishment.

So to promote human flourishing, social policy should be committed to eliminating poverty. But it should also recognise that poverty is just as much a moral condition as a financial one. It must be equally committed to enlarging the scope for freedom and responsibility, rather than narrowing it; increasing the opportunities for people to take ownership of their own lives and rehabilitating those forms of community in which people can care for one another on a more human basis.

Such a policy will necessarily include a role for the state, but it will be one that does not crowd out sources of provision which are closer to people and their communities, and which does not extend to such a degree that it destroys the values of personal responsibility. Indeed, the measure of our social policy's success should not be how many people are dependent on state support, but how many people can meet the challenges of the human condition through their own provision or in combination with others in their family or local community.

The Opportunity of Ownership

Some of the numbers involved in state expenditure on social provision are dizzying, and the complexities of the systems involved lend themselves to inaccessible, technical analysis. But what lies behind that immense growth in state welfare is an unmistakable moral trend that everyone can understand; the increased propensity in our society to pass on responsibility for providing for our basic needs and for people around us onto government. The state is thus consuming a growing proportion of the economy, which is in turn reducing enterprise and industry – the basic fuel of increasing prosperity.

A system of social provision which condemns an ever-growing number of people to dependency on the state is not humane; in fact, it rests upon an ideology which sees humans not as ends in themselves, but mere numbers in the official statistics – passive recipients of cash transfers whose opportunities to take ownership in their lives hardly need to be considered. A social policy conducive to a smaller state, greater prosperity and human flourishing is one based on giving as many people as possible *ownership* over their lives. Fiscally, such a policy will lift an immense burden off our economy. But more importantly, it will greatly expand the possibilities for people to flourish.

6

People, Place and the First-Person Plural

Human beings, in their settled condition, are animated by oikophilia: the love of oikos, which means not only the home but the people contained in it, and the surrounding settlements that endow that home with lasting contours . . . The oikos is the place that is not just mine and yours but ours. It is the stage-set for the first person plural of politics, the locus, both real and imagined, where 'it all takes place'.[1] – Roger Scruton

The danger we have to fear may be roughly summed up in the single word – disintegration. It is the end to which we are being driven, alike by the defective working of our political machinery, and by the public temper of our time.[2] – Lord Salisbury

The First-Person Plural

The liberal rationalist paradigm is animated by a specific theoretical understanding of political authority and obligation – one associated with the social contract theories of the origins of the state that proliferated during the Enlightenment. It holds that men and women were born into a conjectural 'state of nature' with absolute or 'perfect' freedom, and that the forms of association that they enter – and any obligations which they therefore incur – are thus to some degree an alienation of our natural condition.

It holds further that, in the words of John Locke, 'men being, as has been said, by nature, all free, equal, and independent, no one can be put out of this estate, and subjected to the political power of another, without his own consent'.[3] From this conjectural account of man's natural state, liberal rationalists deduce that only those political arrangements which are the product of human reasoning, only those obligations to which we give our consent, are thus legitimate.

But of course, and as numerous philosophers from Hume to Burke and even Bentham have testified, this is not really how humans enter the world at all. We are all born into families, communities and into pre-existing political structures and orders that we do not choose or consent to. And while it need not necessarily or philosophically be the case, we are also – and have since time immemorial been – born into *nations*.

The nation is the contingent community generated by those who share a common geography, a common history, and a common cultural inheritance. It is in the words of Roger Scruton the 'first person plural', the 'we' with which we identify ourselves. It is the communal expression of our inherent 'oikophilia', our love (and our basic need) for home, for place, and for belonging. And it is the vital integrative force in a society comprising a myriad of individuals, families and smaller, proximate forms of community.[4]

Nations are defined by their relationship with place and people. In the first instance, nations have a territoriality. They are confined by a geography, and the people who constitute a nation are bounded together by their common belonging to a particular *place* that they consider as in some way *theirs*. And it is partly by the physical distinctiveness of territoriality that we distinguish one nation from another. This is partly natural and partly architectural. The English countryside – 'criss-crossed by footpaths, green lanes and bridleways' and in which 'copses crown the hills and hedgerows divide the fields' – is distinguishable from the wine regions and rugged mountains of France, which is in turn distinguishable from the topographies of Japan or the United States.[5] But so is the way the built environment in each of these nations have been fashioned and integrated with the natural surroundings. A nation comprises people who recognise themselves as belonging to this territoriality – that it in some way belongs to them, and that they are owners of it.

The nation is not just 'territory' or 'physical locality', however.[6] A collection of individuals who simply happen to live in the same geographical location could hardly be described as constituting a community. A nation, by contrast, is inhabited by a *people*, who have a common story to tell about who they are and their relationship with where they come from – a story expressed through customs and conventions that are learned from those who came before. This makes nations specifically *historical* entities – not simply because they are contingent, but because they are made up of people who share a way of living that has been transmitted through time. This sociocultural dimension to nationhood is essential and ineliminable. Metaphorically, it is the difference between a *national* community and what would effectively be a vast hotel. Inevitably, it was Burke who put it best when he told Parliament that:

> A nation is not only an idea of local extent, and individual momentary aggregation, but it is an idea of continuity which extends in time as well as in numbers and space. And this is a choice not of one day, or of one set of people, not a tumultuary and giddy choice. It is a deliberate election of ages. It is a constitution made by what is ten thousand times better than choice. It is made by the peculiar circumstances, occasions, tempers, dispositions, and moral civil, and social habitudes of the people, which disclose themselves only in a long space of time.[7]

That temporal quality which Burke emphasises is critical to the nation. Its stability and constancy over time is what connects its present members to those who inhabited it before, as well as to those who will do so in the future. And that sense of permanency, that our existence somehow transcends the limited time we physically spend on the Earth, is essential to the security and durability of our identity as individuals.

We experience it when we witness a landscape that has been enjoyed through the ages or participate in a practice or a convention which has been engaged in by successive generations. The nation is, as George Orwell wrote movingly in *The Lion and the Unicorn*, 'continuous, it stretches into the future and the past, there is something in it that persists, as in a living creature'. What can, to paraphrase Orwell, the England of today have in common with the England of 1840? 'But then, what have you in common with the child of five whose photograph your mother keeps on the mantelpiece? Nothing, except that you happen to be the same person.'[8]

Nations are not intrinsic ends in themselves. Their immense value lies in the fact that they are containers of modes of living which have proven themselves to be conducive to flourishing. They are the communal basis of political orders and are thus a chief source of their integrity and cohesion. Which is not to say that they are directed towards achieving some particular end, to which the individual inhabitants are but means. They are not, as Oakeshott put it, 'enterprise' associations, and are justified instead by their proven capacity to support the freedom and responsibility of their members.[9] But they are *prescriptive*; they suggest that certain values and a certain way of life are conducive to flourishing for those that live in a particular place.

Relatedly, the nation is *not* the same thing as the state, though plenty on both the left and the right have conflated or confused the two. 'The state is all we have to act for the "We"', writes Will Hutton.[10] But the state is an artifice, an institution created by human hands and which some would wish to employ as a directing intelligence in society, whereas the nation is an organic expression of a people's shared identity, generated by their common customs, history and locality. It is the product of human action but not design – 'what is ten thousand times better than choice', as Burke put it. It is real too, but not in the sense that it has independent agency.

This is not to say, however, that the state itself does not have a vital and active relationship with the nation. For in its role in transmitting forms of political order that have been conducive to human flourishing, the state has an obligation to preserve the social and cultural continuity of the nation. But the two ought not to be confused, for the impersonal state can never replicate the nation, which is built upon the personal relationships that people develop with others that share the same physical home and a common cultural inheritance.

Loyalty, Trust, Stake

The proper place for human flourishing is at the level of the personal and the local, where human interactions are intimate, and moral agency can have a directness. The wider the social setting, the more abstracted the human interactions, and the more diminished their effects are upon the human character. But we belong to and participate in broader social contexts too, and there are a variety of conditions required for human flourishing that cannot be produced locally. As discussed earlier, the state cannot flourish on our behalf, but it can create the conditions for flourishing. Policing, criminal justice, the rule of law, a decent social safety net, external defence – these are things which must be provided for collectively, which require individuals to make sacrifices for some common good, and for which human societies form themselves into *states*.

In the liberal rationalist perspective, the state can perform these roles and make provision for the collective future of all because of a social contract, whereby rights and obligations are shared on the basis of consent – tacit or explicit. And nothing further than a contractual relationship of exchanged obligations is required for this mutually beneficial arrangement to function. For the advocates of liberal rationalism, such an arrangement is so patently reasonable that any freely acting individual would adopt it. It relies solely upon the vertical relations between state and consenting individuals; liberal rationalists have little to say about the horizontal relations between people within a given society.

This is, however, a hollow conception of how shared political obligations work. For it does nothing to explain why human beings might be prepared to make personal sacrifices for the sake of others in the first place, or why that sense of obligation extends to a specific and limited set of strangers beyond those whom one engages with directly, or why indeed any of this might endure among a group of people in a particular place over time.

In fact, the state is not self-standing. It depends for its functionality on cultural resources which are external to it and sustain it, including the existence of an underlying group identity, which can transcend a people's myriad differences and foster the conviction that they are somehow part of a common whole. For 'people need to identify themselves through a first-person plural if they are to accept the sacrifices required by society'.[11] It is the nation that furnishes this first-person plural and does so in a way that is vastly more tolerant, capacious and resilient than other forms of community identity.

In providing the first-person plural of a people, the nation serves an essential integrative function, because it enables diverse people to consider themselves as in some way coextensive of one another. Ultimately, humans have the capacity to be profoundly generous and altruistic, but as Jonathan Haidt writes, that generosity and altruism is expressed towards those with whom one identifies in some way.[12] Altruism tends to be 'parochial'; it derives from a sense of loyalty, which develops between those who consider themselves to belong to a shared group or community. By identifying with one another, individuals and groups of individuals can come to see their interests as common, and make shared sacrifices in pursuit of them:

> When an individual includes a certain other within the purview of his or her self, we call this attachment *loyalty*. When two individuals have each taken the other under the protection of their extended selves, the bond that is established is one of mutual loyalty, which allows these two individuals to regard themselves as a single entity. The existence of such bonds of mutual loyalty does not mean that they entirely cease to be independent persons. These bonds do not eliminate the competition, insult, jealousy, and quarrels that are always present between individuals who are loyal to one another . . . But as soon as either of them faces adversity, the other suffers this hardship as if it were his own. And in the face of this hardship, the disputes that had troubled them before are temporarily suspended or entirely forgotten.[13]

We see national loyalties at their most intense during moments of external insecurity, when the safety of all is jeopardised by a common threat. It is this that means quite remarkable levels of coordination are possible in wartime. But nations maintain an internal cohesion – that quality that describes the degree to which communities 'maintain their shape under conditions of stress or adversity' – through time and outside of conflict because of a widespread sense of loyalty between individuals who identify themselves with one another.[14]

Common group identity is also generative of trust. Those belonging to the same nation inherit the same dispositions and conventions about certain ethical and behavioural questions, and these produce a set of expectations about their interactions with each other – a confidence that a given act will be met with a reciprocal response. In addition to a common identity, this trust is the fundament of coordinated action to address challenges which may not be soluble in the personal and local context. It also reduces the need for a centralised authority to regulate our behaviour with one another. A high trust society is one in which there is more decentralisation, freer trade and higher productivity.[15] Trust, in the words of sociologist Robert Putnam, reduces the 'transaction costs' of dealing with fellow men and women, and 'lubricate[s] the inevitable frictions of social life'.[16]

Most importantly, nations create a sense of *membership*, of belonging to a group to which one owes duties and from which one derives rights and benefits. And a cohesive, durable polity cannot exist

> without [the] experience of membership. For it is this that enables me to regard the interests and needs of strangers as my concern; that enables me to recognise the authority of decisions and laws that I must obey, even though they are not directly in my interest; that gives me a criterion to distinguish those who are entitled to the benefit of the sacrifices that my membership calls from me, from those who are interloping.[17]

Nations are able to generate a sense of common membership across people of considerable variety and diversity. But while they are malleable – and vastly more so than identity groups based on religious or ethnic qualities – they are not infinitely capacious. Nations are necessarily exclusionary – they must be able to establish which people belong and do not belong to the group, and they must be able to confer rights and privileges on members but not upon others. They define their members by their inhabiting of a particular place, their adoption of a set of practices and customs, and their recognition of a set of basic moral dispositions which they have inherited from others who called that same place home.

That malleability of the nation extends to the fact that it can accommodate people who adopt it as their home, and who can become members of that community on the same terms as anyone else. As such, nations are open to considerable change and growth. But to preserve their cohesion, nations also need to be able to modulate that change so that it takes place 'in deference to the manners, the customs, the laws and the traditions of a people', and does not dislocate the sense of membership which is the nation's essence. Nations must be able to provide a stability of identity over time for people to insulate themselves from the disorientation generated by social change or the creative destruction of economic activity.

In this, the state has a vital role to play in setting conditions on membership, proscribing the duties and responsibilities that people must shoulder if they are to enjoy the benefits of belonging to a given group. Of course, that does not mean that a given country cannot be the temporary home of people who do not wish to become members of that nation, or that its relationship with other nations ought not to be generous and warm. But it does mean that the state has a responsibility to ensure the continuity of whatever it is that makes the nation distinctive, and which safeguards a people's sense of rootedness.

Britain is a union of nations, the core of which is England. It is easy to think of the English national identity as being marked by particular political institutions, by a particular language, and by a particular legal framework. These are all important aspects of Englishness, but really, they are but the upshot of a distinctive sociological *history* that has given England its unique characteristics. For hundreds of years, life in our country has been defined by the existence of small, nuclear families that are mobile, have limited ties to extended family and which have had to look 'outwards' to 'create networks of support and insurance'.[18]

It has been defined, too, by a powerful but limited government that protected these small families from dominating one another and which helped furnish the conditions for them to trade freely. Over generations, this has made for 'a very unusual social and political structure indeed. England has unusually small families, unusually strong national government, unusually weak local magnates, and unusually free peasants'. This structure explains why we set such stall by personal responsibility and civil society, why we embrace a government that is narrow but powerful, why we consider risk-taking important and the building of savings a moral imperative.[19]

This sociological settlement was neither consciously designed and planned, nor consented to at any particular time. But it is quintessentially English, and has historically proven itself to be conducive to the flourishing of people who reside in this place. As such, the state has an interest in maintaining and conserving it. And it has an interest too in maintaining the political community which binds England to the other nations 'nestled' within the territory of the United Kingdom, and whose common identity centres upon not only a fealty to a set of shared political institutions, but also the collective memory of sacrifice in war.[20]

Above all else, nations help to generate that powerful feeling of stake among people in a society – that notion of personal ownership in the collective fortunes of a community to which duties are owed but also from which a sense of belonging and rootedness can be gained, as well as more material advantages. Indeed, the idea that people are owners in a nation which belongs to all its citizens and for which they are responsible is an important driver of collective prosperity too. It is what makes the safety net provided by the welfare system legitimate in the eyes of those who pay for it. It is what enables particular groups to sacrifice a cherished view in the cause of providing badly needed infrastructure, or suffer the inconvenience generated by the construction of new homes. It is what encourages consumers and businesses to engage in the long-term process of building a more productive domestic economy instead of depending on cheaper goods and cheaper labour from abroad in perpetuity.

Liberal Rationalism, Mass Immigration and Multiculturalism

For a number of decades, proponents of the liberal rationalist worldview have been engaged upon a project to destroy the first-person plural generated by the nation. In the first place, this has been stimulated by a disdain for the idea that our mode of social and economic life at all requires external, autonomous, *cultural* structures of support. In fact, economically, the sense of loyalty which binds people from a common nation together represents a form of friction to the liberal rationalist, impairing the smooth operations of markets that are not limited by geography. The natural desire for people to remain in the place they call home, or their preference for domestic industries, represents a 'stickiness' – an economic irrationality that slows the processes of adaptation towards greater market efficiency in trade or labour markets or industry. National loyalties are undesigned, organic and non-rational; they are impediments to building a world that better conforms to the liberal rationalist ideal.

Instances of this way of thinking are abundant today. In his brilliant *The Road to Somewhere*, David Goodhart recounts a conversation he had with the former Cabinet Secretary Gus O'Donnell, who argued that his job as Britain's chief civil servant was to 'maximise global welfare and not national welfare'.[21] But perhaps inevitably the anti-nation case *par excellence* is most often made in the columns of *The Guardian*. National loyalties are 'absurd', argues Philippe Sands – we are all 'citizens of the world' and ought to have global passports.[22] 'England means nothing to me', wrote George Monbiot in another representative article: 'I consider myself a global citizen – a member of the species – before I consider myself a national citizen. I believe that everyone has an equal entitlement to the world's wealth and power. I don't love England, but nor do I hate it. I am *indifferent*.'[23]

But it is not just a negligence or disregard for the role of the nation that has defined the liberal rationalist position. It is an active antagonism too. For the nation generates obligations that are not freely chosen and imposes duties upon newcomers that are both demanding and prescriptive. These are irreconcilable with a worldview that sees the highest purpose of politics as being the absolute liberation of the individual from such constraints.

The nation embodies the idea that rights are fused to responsibilities. By belonging to a national community, citizens derive certain advantages and protections. We all benefit from a system of support and welfare that protects those who fall on hard times – a system which is the material expression of national solidarity, of a people's commitment to supporting those to whom they are loyal. But to gain those advantages, an individual is expected to fulfil certain duties too: to provide for oneself as far as possible, to learn the history and customs of the people who built the society that they have inherited, to make one's own contribution towards the support of others. The synthesis of rights and responsibilities is what constitutes citizenship and provides the sense of stake that is the lifeforce of all communities.

Liberal rationalism is hostile to this basic idea. It sees rights and responsibilities as diametrically opposed, such that an increase in a person's responsibilities necessitates a decrease in their freedoms. Unchosen obligations to a way of life inherited from the past limit the ability of the individual to think or do or say what they want in the present. Loyalty to nation minimises the ability of individuals to move and contract freely. Liberal rationalism encourages us to reject the idea of thinking about politics from the perspective of nations entirely. Its unit of analysis and indeed its ideal political actor is the deracinated individual, thinking freely and rationally about how best to satisfy their desires. And in this, it is predisposed towards the interests of those who David Goodhart has called the 'Anywheres' – highly mobile individuals whose identities are 'portable', whose ability to derive benefit from the globalised economy is strong, and whose national loyalties are weak.[24]

This perspective also gives liberal rationalism its internationalism. Politically, it sees no moral reason why the interests of those around the world who might wish to reside in Britain should not be treated as on a parity with those who already live here. All who wish ought to be able to reside in Britain without corresponding duties, and they should be at liberty to retain or adopt whatever customs or conventions they desire. In fact, as Eric Kaufmann has contended, this actually lends an asymmetry to the liberal rationalist position: the interests of newcomers to Britain to choose their modes of living trumps the desire of existing citizens to maintain and preserve a cultural inheritance that they believe distinguishes the people who live in this specific place.[25]

Largely, these perverse perspectives stem from liberal rationalism's own peculiar understanding of human nature. It believes that trust, generosity and warmness for strangers is universal, or even less credibly, that these things are a function of economic development: that 'people are more tolerant of diversity and immigration as they grow more confident about becoming richer. As the economy grows there are resources for improved public services; altruism and generosity expand as horizons broaden.'[26] Just how divorced this view is from a proper understanding of how people and communities interact is a point that need not be laboured. But it is this sort of liberal complacency which has fostered negligence towards a common national identity.

This erosion of the first-person plural is being driven by two related trends encouraged by liberal rationalism, the first of which are the present levels of immigration. There is a commonplace belief that the British Isles have accommodated constant demographic upheaval throughout history, and that 'her destiny', as G. M. Trevelyan put it, has continually been decided by those entering the country from outside – 'by the boat-crews which . . . floated to her shore'.[27]

Such a self-conception is inevitably tied to a particular understanding of the country's imperial past too – with the British Isles at the core of a transnational network of population movement. But as Trevelyan argues, for about a millennium after the Norman Conquest, Britain was characterised in fact by relative demographic stability over time, combining 'a slow, peaceful infiltration' of new people 'with the acquiescence of the existing inhabitants of the island'.[28]

Britain was remarkably effective at assimilating this level of population change. Over 70 per cent of British DNA at the end of the Second World War dated back more than 6,000 years on the British Isles.[29] The British population has shown 'extraordinary stability' since 600 AD, the Oxford Geneticist Professor Sir Walter Bodmer has written. In such a context, past immigration did in fact conform to the image that many of the liberal disposition have of it: as a source of energy, vigour, talent and advancement. Newcomers were integrated and assimilated, adopted inherited customs and conventions, assumed responsibilities and developed loyalties to those who shared the territory of these isles. At the same time, our society created the conditions for their flourishing. Within these parameters, immigration certainly was to the inestimable advantage of this country.

In this historical relief, the mass immigration that characterises population flows into Britain over recent decades is entirely unprecedented. From 1855 – as far back as comprehensive statistics go – until the 1990s, Britain was a country characterised by net emigration, not net immigration. This only really began to change after the election of Tony Blair in 1997, with net migration passing 100,000 per annum for the first time ever in 1998. In the twenty-seven years since Blair's election, net migration has directly added 7.33 million people to the population of the UK; in the preceding twenty-seven years, it added 17,000 in total.[30]

The post-2020 wave of immigration has made the break with the past even more dramatic. There was a gross inflow of about 4.5 million people over the 2021–4 period via legal migration routes, reaching a peak of 1.3 million people in the year to December 2023. Net migration for this period is an estimated 2.65 million people – equivalent to 4 per cent of the prior population, or two cities the size of Birmingham. In other words, one in every twenty-five people now living in Britain today has arrived in just the last four years.[31]

All of this has had a transformative impact on the British population. The proportion of residents in England and Wales who were born overseas was 4.3 per cent in 1951. Fifty years later, it was 8.9 per cent. By 2021, the most recent census, it was 16.8 per cent. Given trends since, and population projections by the Office for National Statistics, this will reach around 24 per cent by the time of the next census in 2031, and 33 per cent by 2051.[32] The proportion of second-generation migrants is also set to more than double from around 5 per cent of the population to roughly one in every ten people. These are transformative population shifts.

For the citizen, 'borders are the spatial expression of the bonds of mutual loyalty that hold nations together'. But in the liberal rationalist worldview, border control, and a normative view on an appropriate rate of demographic change in Britain, represent irrational constraints on the free movement of people. More pressingly, they are potential inhibitors of the mass immigration required to sustain our consumptionist economic model. Indeed, with this end of maximising present consumption in mind, the very scale of immigration is liberal rationalism's *intention*. Through the vast importation of people from overseas, Britain might reduce the cost of labour and inject a short-term stimulant into the economy in the form of higher aggregate demand.

Mass immigration also helps to alleviate one of the other key symptoms of liberal rationalism's short-termism and its assault on obligation and responsibility – that is, the decline of family formation and diminishing birth rates. In the 1960s, women of childbearing age each had, on average, just shy of three children. That number has fallen to around 1.4 now, and well below the replacement rate of 2.1.[33] Fewer people are having smaller families, as raising children is seen as increasingly economically unviable, an undesirable responsibility or constraint on personal freedom, or both.

In aggregate terms, and with people living longer into old age, we are failing to produce enough young people of working age to generate the tax receipts that fund the services which the elderly are drawing upon. Immigration is turned to as an alternative means of providing a sufficient working population to sustain those in retirement and requiring support. But it is no real solution, since it does nothing to address the underlying causes of this demographic dilemma: our inability as a country to have enough children.

The second trend is related to the first. If mass immigration is the quantitative dimension of liberal rationalism's attack on nationhood, *multiculturalism* is its qualitative counterpart. Partly a consequence of the view that political and economic arrangements or regimes do not require specific cultural foundations, partly a necessary response to a scale of immigration that prohibits a serious approach to assimilation and integration, multiculturalism has defined the political consensus on what a good society looks like in the twenty-first century. It is in effect a policy of cultural relativism – the view that all cultures are equivalents of one another and should be treated as such.

In practice, multiculturalism is also a policy of *repudiation* – the rejection of the idea that a nation can have a dominant or majority culture that it has a right to maintain and promote.[34] Multiculturalism is in tension with assimilation, for while the former seeks the preservation of diverse cultures for the sake of diversity itself, the latter involves some conforming of the values and practices of newcomers to the culture of the place they are adopting.

Multiculturalism rejects the idea that national identities are exclusionary categories. It sees nations as mere territories and not as culturally prescriptive, and therefore as infinitely capacious of different cultures and ways of life. It is why advocates of multiculturalism often display a radical antipathy towards the teaching of a national history and equate progress with the erasure of those marks of cultural distinctiveness. 'If Britain is to become what it can be', writes Will Hutton, 'a progressive, front-rank European power with a vigorous economy and fair society, committed to European peace and the achievement of net zero – it can no longer be trapped by its past.'[35]

In fact, it goes further and asserts that diversity *in and of itself* is the source of a society's strength. This thought is latent in much liberal political philosophy, and can be found in the Madisonian principle that the stability and success of the polity is best guaranteed by the 'multiplicity of factions', through which ambition may be made to counteract ambition.[36] Economically, it is argued, diversity also promotes innovation, better decision-making in executive bodies, and openness to change. The irony is that multiculturalism has actually produced its own monoculture, a sort of 'homogeneous diversity', which asserts that difference is everywhere and always desirable, and which in turn kills the real variety of community life. Every business, every civil society group, every association is increasingly expected to demonstrate their commitment to diversity, equity and inclusion; but the more they do so, the more they begin to look the same.[37]

Difference itself is not the source of a society's strength, however. Nations do not function well because they promote diversity, but because they are able to maintain some powerful, underlying sense of unity even among diverse people. In fact, whereas nationhood generates trust and cooperation, diversity does precisely the opposite, encouraging people to withdraw, and 'pull in like a turtle'.[38] Strong nations can be diverse; but it is not their diversity which makes them strong. This is the difference between multiculturalism and *pluralism*. The latter describes a society in which a range of communities can coexist *because* they defer to a common culture, language and history, whereas the former denotes an amorphous set of groups which rejects such a deference and finds itself fragmenting in consequence.

None of this is an argument against diversity itself. It's an argument against diversity when it comes at the expense of that thing which enables a society composed largely of strangers to cohere and coexist peacefully. Nor does it require different cultures from across the world to be placed into some ranking. It is instead a defence of *particularism* – the notion that particular cultures are fitted for particular peoples and places – that the customs, conventions and sociological patterns of Britain are unique, have emerged organically, and are worth energetically preserving because they have proved conducive to human flourishing.[39]

Disintegration

The combined effects of mass immigration and multiculturalism have been stark. Together, they have contributed to the same moral and social deconstruction that we have been examining. The vast importation of people in a short space of time, particularly in cities, with little attention as to how they might become integrated members of the wider community of responsibility to others, has created a sense of fracture with the organic development of society – of a radical break with how this country has previously managed population change in order to preserve and maintain its historical continuity. And the policy of multiculturalism – in its default assumption that diversity is and always must be beneficial – has ensured that many newcomers have not been afforded the cultural grammar with which they might gain a genuine stake in our national life.

For the advocates of the levels of immigration Britain has witnessed in recent decades, it is intrinsically good and humane to allow anyone and everyone who wishes to reside in this country to do so. It allows people to pursue a better life for their family, or for the persecuted to find refuge. There is undoubtedly truth in these claims – and an immigration policy which facilitates such immigration while preserving the historical continuity of the nation that they are adopting would be to the benefit of both host country and migrant.

But the present *mass* model of immigration is neither good nor humane. In fact, it is precisely the opposite. It cares little for those coming to this country as *persons* who to flourish have sociocultural requirements, and who ought to be properly integrated into a place which they can call home. They are instead simply numbers, extra consumers and producers to be included in the economic statistics, and who will lend a veneer of healthiness to annual GDP figures.

Mass and uncontrolled immigration is also destructive of the idea of organic community itself. That is why control over borders is so important. For as Alexander Rüstow once wrote, 'the self-evident and unavoidable prerequisite for any social group with a communal character is that a new member can enter it only with the approval of those already belonging to it. Once this right of co-optation is abolished . . . its communal character is destroyed.'[40] The abolition of borders transforms a national community based on shared loyalty and obligation into an undifferentiated mass of individuals who happen to exist in the same geographical location.

Mass immigration and multiculturalism promote the 'massification' of society, by which it loses 'the inner and organic character of the genuine and spontaneous community', is deprived of its sociological structure, and comes to resemble 'a mere sandheap of individuals'.[41] The feeling of mutual obligation – that my neighbour is somehow an extension of myself and thus their interests are in some way my own – which begets loyalty is damaged. And this in turn reduces the legitimacy of burden sharing within society.

We see this with welfare, and the animosity towards the idea that taxpayers are subsidising the existence of people who do not share corresponding responsibilities and duties. But it is also acute in the debate around the provision of new housing, for example, as communities become reluctant to support development that will inevitably have disruptive consequences for them, and which they have come to believe will only help sustain the present model of mass immigration that is altering the place they call home without any sense of purpose or control.

Mass immigration also further encourages the short-termism that characterises liberal rationalism. By fracturing the sense of a nation's historical continuity, mass immigration erodes the sense that the present generation has intertemporal duties – to take what has been inherited from previous generations, maintain it, and pass it on to future ones. As Patrick Deneen has argued, when the conviction that we belong to a historically continuous community or partnership is lost, the propensity to think about what will improve the long-term prosperity of our country is lost too.[42] Investment, saving, even the desire to have families and raise children – all seem less important in a society which exists only for the present. Mass immigration, as Ed West has written, 'is a form of social debt, offering small-term financial benefits with long-term social costs to future generations'.[43]

It fractures the idea of citizenship too. Citizens bear responsibilities, just as much as they enjoy rights. But *mass* immigration, combined with insufficient policies to promote integration, gives the impression that no such responsibilities are incurred by those joining the national community. Newcomers can benefit from the security and prosperity of residing in a particular place without adopting the practices or principles of the historical and cultural enterprise that made those collective goods possible. That dislocation of rights from responsibilities is the very object of liberal rationalism. But it is one of the central causes of reduced trust and cohesion – the social goods that enable people to make shared sacrifices for a common goal.

Finally, our present model of mass immigration is intimately tied up with the burgeoning size of the state. We have already seen in the previous chapter how the state depends on high levels of immigration to keep its wage bill low. But mass immigration and statism form part of the same cohesive scheme. Without the 'genuine' integration that is offered through belonging to a shared national community, the state is increasingly required to foster a 'pseudo-integration' – one based not upon the ties of loyalty between people who identify with one another, but upon the authority of the state.[44]

Additionally, the very size of the state and its willingness to offer rights to newcomers without imposing responsibilities is itself a driver of mass immigration. Mass migration and statism thus exhibit a symbiotic relationship. A larger state with more generous welfare provision is a pull factor for those in countries with less generous, 'strings attached' systems, while the proportion of people who immigrate from abroad that are likely to be net beneficiaries – rather than contributors – increases demand for state support.[45]

The residents of this country both new and established are increasingly *not* citizens with a sense of ownership of the fortunes of their country. They are rather undifferentiated particles, a sandheap of individuals, tightly packed together but lacking in anything durable to bind them together. A *crowd*, not a *people*. Devitalised, demoralised and without a personal sense of responsibility for the place to which they belong, their willingness to make personal sacrifices for some object beyond the satisfaction of their immediate desires is greatly weakened. The vital impulses which motivate decision-making in the interest of long-term prosperity are thus diminished, and more and more individuals look to the state to provide the cohesion that was formerly provided organically through nationhood.

In effect, as our collective first-person plural has eroded, we have been asking the state to substitute for the nation in providing the people with some form of social solidarity. Instead, its role ought to be the maintenance of the nation as a vital source of cohesion, and as a historical repository of conventions, customs and modes of living that have proven themselves to be well adapted to this country. The welfare state is no longer the political expression of an authentic social solidarity contained within the nation. It is, rather, becoming the only thing that we collectively have in common. And in its injustices and inequities, it is now beginning to drive us apart, not bring us together.

Reversing these trends, rebuilding a sense of loyalty and shared obligation, will require a renewal of the first-person plural. It will require us to generate again that sense of stake in the national community among those who live here which is the essence of citizenship. Only through doing this can we rediscover those instincts that enable a society of millions who lack direct personal relationships to make sacrifices for one another.

A Nation of Owners

As Danny Kruger has written, it is by getting right a set of personal relationships – with our friends and family, with our neighbourhood, with our local community, with our civil associations – that we shall begin to restore our society to health.[46] At this level, people can develop a more acute sense of responsibility and obligation to others, and take ownership of their lives. Much of this book has been an argument for the principle of subsidiarity – that 'a community of a higher order should not interfere in the internal life of a community of a lower order [thus] depriving the latter of its functions', because this strips society of its 'human energies' and promotes the development of inhuman bureaucracies.[47] That principle of subsidiarity is a key tenet of the personalist worldview, in which moral life is lived at the local and human level. And it is why the case presented herein is so sceptical of the state annexing an ever-growing range of functions and competencies.

But we do participate in wider networks and associations, and the activities and interests of our many local communities must be integrated to promote general flourishing. The nation has served that vital, integrative role effectively and informally, underwriting our ability to make sacrifices for those who share this country, but whom we cannot know intimately. It stems from a bottom-up loyalty that emerged organically, rather than one that is imposed from above. It is a powerful, very real source of belonging for those that live in this place and have inherited its culture. In its absence, the hard and impersonal power of the state will become more necessary to provide order.

The experiences of shared sacrifice in the conflicts of the last century which fostered our national solidarity are increasingly distant, and so their binding effect has diminished over time. At the same time, the centrifugal effects of liberal rationalist dogmas on our approach to culture and community have further intensified the sense of disintegration and fragmentation. But the story of our first-person plural does not have to be told 'in elegiac accents'.[48] Our nation is what we make of it. And by giving people a stake, a sense of ownership in a national community of which they can be proud, we can glue our society back together again and take steps to restore the trust and the feelings of responsibility and obligation that are essential for society to prosper.

7

What Is to Be Done?

We put too much faith in systems, and look too little to men.[1] – Benjamin Disraeli

Decentralisation of administration is not merely feasible technically; it is a prime necessity of free culture.[2] – Robert Nisbet

Homeostatic Solutions

The preceding chapters have sought to explain a profound transformation that has taken place in Britain, and what the consequences of all this have been for our society and economy. Now, in this final chapter, it is time to consider what we ought to do about this situation.

Liberal rationalism has created a culture in which whenever we are confronted with some problem to be overcome, we look first to government. What I have argued for is a sea change in how we think about social challenges; for us to see the task of building a better society not as the responsibility of the abstract state, but as *our* challenge, and thus *your and my* challenge.[3] We need to forge an *ownership society*, and a politics that nurtures the capacity of individuals, families and communities to maintain themselves, rather than one that erodes that capacity.

The shoots of such a politics are visible today, be it in campaign group Looking for Growth's efforts to clean up the graffiti on London Underground trains, or the remarkable surge in volunteering during the coronavirus pandemic. It can be seen at a hyper-local level too, in organisations like the Vale Pantry – a social supermarket in North Dorset – or the Keswick Community Land Trust, which has enabled the construction of high-quality affordable housing on former church land in the Lake District. These shoots need to be tended to and helped to grow.

With all that said, our current political framework does not generally permit this sort of organic problem-solving whereby, like self-regulating systems in nature, groups of people are able to develop solutions spontaneously.[4] In fact, it actively undermines it. For conservatives, this poses a dilemma – conservatism is traditionally sceptical about using government to shape society. But this scepticism has hardened into an anti-political tendency, leaving conservatives today unwilling to change a status quo that is deeply hostile to the values they champion.

Yes, we must avoid the mistake of simply developing a 'conservative rationalism' to oppose liberal rationalism – a policy of continued government tinkering but with alternative outcomes in mind. However, it must be recognised that even if conservatives might wish to be uninterested in politics, politics remains interested in *us*. While culture underpins and influences policy, politics can in turn shape culture. Government cannot, as liberals would have us believe, be impartial or disinterested about the basic normative framework that makes our way of life possible. It must actively nurture it. Liberal disinterestedness is its own positive expression of values, and it has done great damage to our country.

If we want a society in which people are freer to flourish in association with others, we first need politicians with conviction and courage to construct a framework in which that is possible.

If we wish to build an ownership society, we need politicians prepared to take ownership themselves.

In what follows, I offer some concrete policy suggestions for how we might begin to repatriate responsibility, push society's centre of gravity downwards, and create the conditions for more people to prosper and flourish.

Given the wide coverage of subjects in this chapter, some considerations of policy design have been omitted in an effort not to totally overwhelm the reader. Ultimately, my object at the end of this book is to show how and where the values of ownership can be proactively encouraged, not to produce a government white paper. For while it seems that the technical proficiency of policymaking has continued to improve significantly, I believe that our understanding of how policies interact with culture is as impoverished as it has ever been. Addressing that lack of understanding is my principal concern here.

Political Responsibility and the Cincinnatus State

I have argued that what we need in Britain is a 'Cincinnatus state' – one which supports the forms of association and moral values that would make its presence unnecessary in certain areas of social life. The ethic of ownership has been so damaged that we now need government to play a role in reviving it. Much of that role will be the strategic transfer of social functions to the private sphere of individuals, families, communities and businesses, and a more proactive effort to rehabilitate those forms of association which would substitute for the state.

But there is an issue that must be addressed before any of this is possible: the power of *elected* politicians has been so diminished that the state itself has become unresponsive to attempts to change or reform it. The immense expansion in the state's functions has *not* produced more effective or responsive democratic government, and that is because the growth of the latter has largely come at the expense of the former, as the power of elected representatives has given way to the power of state *bureaucracy*.

Our elected representatives themselves have been entirely complicit in this transfer. They too have been driven by the same desire to absolve themselves of responsibility, and many of them have also been convinced that political questions are technical in nature, and thus better addressed by 'experts'.

Politicians have come to think that by ceding responsibility for making difficult decisions and potentially contentious trade-offs, they might somehow secure better outcomes. Others thought, as Pete Burnham argued, that they would be 'insulated from the political consequences of notionally unpopular policies'.[5] What they have all discovered is that in ceding responsibility, they have in turn also conceded power – power which they were never entitled to give away.

Britain's inherited constitutional settlement was imbued with the moral values and cultural dispositions that have been the subject of this book. It was animated by the idea that responsibility should be as direct, and lines of accountability as clear as possible; it is why Parliament operates on the basis of constituency MPs, to preserve the link between core and periphery. In its sovereignty, Parliament had great latitude to act and decide, but this was balanced by an ultimate accountability to the public.

That same line of accountability ran through to government. Ministers were accountable to Parliament and could govern only so long as they maintained its confidence. Ministers *owned* their departmental briefs and could effectively exercise the power that they had been provisionally vested with. But when they failed in their portfolio, they took responsibility for their decisions. Ours was a *political* constitution. It gave government power and agency, but responsibility too.

For decades, though, our politicians have been busily giving away powers that were properly invested in them by the public. This started with the rise of regulators and arm's-length bodies from the 1980s, but was given impetus and drive by New Labour after 1997, and regrettably by Conservative governments since. A system based on parliamentary sovereignty, with the executive placed within and accountable to the legislature, has been replaced. Border policy is determined by domestic and European Courts, not the elected government. Bodies like the Climate Change Committee determine our planning and energy policies, preventing our representatives from making judgements between competing political imperatives. And across Whitehall, the direction of government is determined just as much by the vast number of policy advisors within the civil service as it is by ministers. Our constitution now seems almost deliberately structured to diminish the sense of responsibility required for accountable government.

In order to push power downwards, we first need politicians to recover it from the bodies that they have carelessly ceded it to – courts foreign and domestic, regulators, and the state bureaucracy. Until we do this, the sort of societal renewal that this book envisages will be impossible.

Firstly, the law. The litany of legislative acts that take decision-making powers which ought to rest with Parliament and hand them to the courts – including the Equality Act, the Human Rights Act and the Climate Change Act – must be repealed or reformed. The issue, of course, is not the substance of what each act ostensibly promotes. Reduced discrimination, the upholding of fundamental rights and the reduction of the harm we do to the environment are all notionally laudable objectives. The issue at stake is *who* gets to decide how these objectives ought to be pursued. And in this, these acts share a common ideological core: a belief that it should be lawyers, 'experts' in particular fields, who choose, not the elected.

Secondly, regulatory reform. The number of regulators should be drastically pared back, and those retained should be issued with sunset clauses and a statutory period within which their performance and remit is reviewed by Parliament. The wide use of 'skeleton' bills or clauses – bits of legislation so vague that they in practice give wide powers of interpretation to agencies and delegated bodies – must be ended.

Finally, the permanent bureaucracy. The civil service needs to be significantly pared back in size, at least to the pre-pandemic headcount. Ministers should then be given greater room to seek their own legal and political counsel from appointed advisors, rather than relying on advisors given to them by the civil service itself.

All of this will enable the government to start exercising powers that are properly entrusted to it by the public – most importantly, the hard powers of defence, justice and security. Domestically, we must end our culture of permissiveness within our criminal justice system, invest heavily in prison capacity and neighbourhood policing, and empower the police to use methods – like stop and search – with a proven record of reducing crime. Sentencing guidelines should see prolific offenders issued with a mandatory minimum custodial sentence.

Equally, we need to take ownership for the defence of the realm again. A dramatic increase in defence investment is required, particularly in our conventional capabilities, as well as more day-to-day spending on a larger armed forces. British soldiers who bravely serve their country on operations must also be provided assurances that they will not be hounded later in life for doing so by activist lawyers.

Taken together, these measures will begin to restore the vital chain that ought to link governor to governed. It will see elected politicians take back responsibility from unelected bureaucracies. And from here, a reforming government can start to meaningfully devolve power downwards.

The Property-Owning Democracy

The material basis of a programme for restoring ownership in Britain would be a vast distribution of property. But wider property ownership is not the sole end; what we need to promote is the forms of property ownership that best inculcate responsibility, a long-term perspective, and a sense of stake in society and the economy.

The entire operating logic of our fiscal and economic policy needs to be reversed to deliver this diffusion of property. Our approach for some time has been to accept a relatively static distribution of property ownership, and to compensate for this through ever-rising levels of progressive taxation. In fact, we need precisely the opposite approach: to proactively seek to widen the opportunities for property ownership while pursuing a tax policy aimed at raising sufficient revenues for specified services rather than wealth redistribution.

Politics is about applying enduring principles to changed circumstances. How do we apply the principles of a property-owning democracy set out by Noel Skelton one hundred years ago to the circumstances of today? I propose five policies to increase ownership in a range of different assets, but also to encourage a particular type of ownership too.

First, fiscal reform. As a clear sign that fiscal policy will no longer be intended principally to redistribute the proceeds of wealth but to fund specific services, all marginal rates above 50 per cent should be eliminated, such that the earner is always the majority owner in each £1 of income that they earn.[6]

Second, home ownership. Being able to own a home of one's own continues to be the most instinctive and deeply held aspiration for the majority of British households. But our narrow treatment of housing as an investment good the real value of which must be allowed to rise perpetually has undercut its moral function – as a medium for moral development and a source of self-sufficiency that should be attainable for all willing to work hard in life.

We will need both demand- and supply-side interventions to address collapsing home ownership rates among the young. In the case of the former, this means a vast reduction in annual immigration, which is putting a strain on all forms of housing, and will be considered below. But the other main obstacle to home ownership at present is an insufficient supply of well-designed homes, especially in urban areas.

Our state-led planning system needs to be transformed so that it is not merely easier to build, but easier to build *well*. Our current system does the opposite: the thicket of rules and regulations deters smaller, often locally based builders and leaves larger housebuilders as the only game in town. Almost a third of all new homes delivered in 2024 were built by just five developers, which is why we see the same cookie-cutter developments that start crumbling within a matter of years plonked alongside our neighbourhoods.

We need to radically scale back the regulatory burden on small to medium-sized developments – including on things like biodiversity net gain or the requirement to make on-site social housing provision – so that locally based builders can start to compete again. Automatic approval should be given for certain types of urban densification within city limits via Local Development Orders.

And the government should put its support behind a new generation of garden villages. These would need to be proposed by locally elected authorities, and they should count towards any housing delivering obligations they are currently under. But we should be ambitious about these projects; they should engage local builders, come with the highest design standards and be built not merely as vast housing estates, but as communities in which people can develop a sense of stake and belonging. The work of the Duchy of Cornwall in Poundbury provides inspiration for what is possible.

Third, leasehold and freehold reform. There are too many instances today when people pick up the keys to their new home or flat under the impression that they have finally acquired a measure of economic independence and security, only to find out that they are subject to service charges and fees over which they have no control. Leasehold in the present system is a simulation of ownership, not the real thing. And the thousands of people caught up in the 'fleecehold' scandal, in which they purchase a home on a new estate but are subject to the arbitrary decisions of a private management company, are in the same situation. This undermines the idea of ownership itself.

It is welcome that the government intends to ban leasehold tenure for future developments. Additionally, however, in future and existing developments, it should be made much simpler for residents to take on the responsibilities for managing their building on a compulsory basis. This ought to apply on housing estates too. For all new estates with a private management company, residents should automatically receive representation and voting rights on financial decision-making.

Fourth, profit-sharing. Any new energy generation or storage infrastructure which comes with a local community benefit agreement should go through an expedited planning pathway. The community benefit agreement would have to be agreed with a local representative organisation like a parish or town council or a community land trust, and would give them a share in the asset. The proceeds could then be paid in the form of a dividend to local residents, or retained and invested in local projects. The main point is that it would be subject to local governance.

Finally, employee ownership schemes. Promoting wider property ownership and a responsible, more future-oriented society is not just a task for government. Businesses have a role to play too. They can create a workforce of mere wage-earners, or of employee-owners with a genuine sense of stake in the way their company is managed. Evidence of the connection between widespread ownership and economic dynamism is ample; employee-owned businesses are about 10 per cent more productive than non-employee-owned firms, and they are also more likely to invest in research and development, skills and training.[7]

Business leaders should take it upon themselves to give not just senior managers stocks in their firms, but as many employees as possible through things like Employee Ownership Trusts and Share Incentive Plans – schemes which provide tax advantages to companies giving their employees shares in the firm. The allowances for these schemes could be increased to encourage wider uptake. Indeed, diffusing share ownership to improve business productivity might be a powerful new mission for Britain's private equity firms to adopt.

Devolving Fiscal Responsibility

The foundation of a system in which individuals, families and associations can take ownership of their social provision is a wholesale devolution of fiscal responsibility. We need to reduce the tax burden, give people more control over their finances, and encourage forms of saving that will enable people to provide for themselves, for their loved ones, and for those around them.

Some preliminary steps ought to be taken in the short term to get a hold of fiscal policy. First, we need to increase the number of people with an interest in lowering the tax burden and spreading financial responsibility. One of the greatest mistakes of Conservative governments since 2010 has been to deliberately take more people out of paying tax by increasing the personal allowance threshold. Such a policy means fewer people with a stake in the fiscal system, and with the sense of responsibility that comes from being financially liable for higher taxes. Tax policy henceforth must seek to broaden the base and hence create incentives for tax rates to be reduced.

We also need to address the fiscal irresponsibility within our pension system by removing the 'triple lock' and indexing state pensions to average earnings growth, thus establishing a stronger connection between the scale of provision and our ability to pay for it. In addition, the retirement age should be raised to 70 more quickly than under existing government proposals. This course will not decrease the burden of the state pension, but it will mean that it grows more slowly, and with more people in work and paying taxes, this might also support the wider economy.

Beyond these preliminary measures, more radical reforms are required to how we save and fund social services. The main policy lever by which we can begin to give people back control and responsibility will be national insurance contributions. Over a period, these should be scrapped. These savings for taxpayers should be used for two things: to build an insurance system for long-term care, and to create the space for higher pensions savings.

Firstly, social care. After the age of, say, 40, people should pay insurance premiums into a dedicated mutual fund. The fund would be independent of the state, owned by contributors, and topped up by employer contributions and state subsidies for the premiums of lower earners.[8] After retirement, anyone should be able to draw on care provision subject to a needs test. Crucially, support ought to be available as services *or* cash in kind. For families that want to care for their loved ones in old age, the cash support available should be generous. Such a system would incentivise at-home or community care, as well as the development of a more mature market in providers.

Ultimately, healthcare too ought to be moved towards a more hybrid system with an insurance component. It should be modelled on the internationally admired and high-performing Dutch system, with strong government oversight and universal coverage, but also mandatory insurance with an annual excess, co-payments for selected services, and competition among insurers and providers – alongside subsidies for those with long-term or high-cost conditions, and free provision for children. There would then be a tax rebate for the cost of the insurance premiums. But we should focus on proving that the insurance model works for social care before attempting such reforms in healthcare.

In the here and now, we could consider direct ways in which people can be incentivised to take greater ownership for their health and well-being upstream. Gym membership, preventative health schemes like screenings, smoking cessation programmes – private insurers already use these initiatives to offer lower premiums, and we should consider ways to scale such programmes. There should also be tax relief for people taking out private health insurance, and in so doing reduce their demand on state resources.

Finally, the state pension. Some proportion of people's national insurance contributions should be moved into a mandatory and contributory personal pension account. Sir Nicholas Lyons has suggested that with annually invested contributions and compounding returns, the government could aim to achieve a fully funded state pension by 2075. And in such a system, it really would be taxpayers contributing towards their own future provision. Savings from ending the triple lock and the increased retirement age could be used to ease the transition, and ensure that young people are not paying for both their own future provision as well as that of current pensioners. This move should be partnered with higher, tax-free auto-enrolment contributions to private pension plans.

The intellectual core of all these various proposals is the same: to get people to take more ownership in their lives – by insuring for the unforeseeable health and care costs they might face, and via savings for the foreseeable costs they will be required to meet in retirement.

Working Age Benefits

The interventions above will lead to a reduction in taxation. Yet most of them will be offset to some degree by an increase in personal insurance contributions. There are, however, welfare reforms for working age benefits that would achieve direct savings for taxpayers.

We saw earlier, for example, how the cost of health-related benefits is going to soar to £100 billion by 2030 without intervention and how this is primarily being driven by an unsustainable surge in people claiming these benefits. *One in every ten people* in the UK is now claiming a sickness or disability benefit; the government estimates that the number of people claiming PIP *alone* will grow to 4.2 million by the end of the decade.[9] Urgent action is required to stem this exponential rise in dependency.

PIP should be reserved for those whose cost of living is materially increased by their disability, and the criteria for this should be tightened. It should be made a conditional benefit with requirements to volunteer, partake in further education or training, or to enter formal employment, and with a narrow set of exemptions for those with the most serious illnesses or conditions.[10]

When it comes to incapacity benefits (payments for those out of work), we are getting things back to front. As it stands, these benefits support those with mental health issues to be out of work, but there is strong evidence to suggest that being out of work is poor for mental health. Incapacity benefits should not be seen as a default option for those with mental health difficulties. Indeed, the worst thing we could be doing for individuals with such challenges is removing them from workplaces or training or educational settings.

In future, eligibility for incapacity benefits should by default be assessed in person, and there should be periodic reassessment of benefit eligibility for those of working age. People on state support ought never to feel that they have been given up on. Instead, we should give those with mental health challenges opportunities to take control in their lives again. The government should support workplace and occupational health schemes so that workers can be better supported without having to leave their employment.

Every effort should be made to give people independence if possible. Reforming disability and incapacity benefits is not about denying support to those who will unavoidably need it. It is about restoring dignity, purpose and opportunity to as many people as possible. If we are to build a humane welfare state, it must serve not only to protect people, but also to empower them to live well.

Social Pluralism

As we devolve fiscal responsibility downwards, we need to encourage and support those forms of association that could provide alternatives to state provision. State-sponsored pluralism – in which government actively tries to support organisations that can substitute for it – will unlock the forces of voluntarism and localism in the delivery of a range of social functions. Some of these alternative providers may well be for-profit companies delivering health or social care. But many others will be mutual aid associations, charities and community groups. The benefit of moving to the insurance system as detailed above is that people would have choice over which providers they use. The state would still play a major part in the system; it would simply cease to be the sole provider of social functions.

One of the most vital functions that the state undertakes is to determine how we use land. Its power is currently total and absolute. Every change of land of use, barring some very specific exceptions, requires express permission from the government, usually at a local level. We should shift the centre of gravity in the planning system away from the state and towards communities by supporting community land trusts (CLTs) – cooperatives that own and manage land within communities.

A significant proportion of new development should be delivered via these organisations. Neighbourhood regeneration funding should be set aside to support the CLTs to make their first land acquisition, permission in principle should be granted to all CLT planning applications, and the 'New Homes Bonus' should be augmented to provide an incentive for homes built on community-owned land. Even more radically, the 1947 Town and Country Planning Act could be reformed so that CLTs are able to give planning permission for land use changes on land they own.

Parishes, once the administrative and spiritual core of communities up and down the country, have been in a state of retreat since the 1930s. But they still contribute billions of pounds' worth of services like counselling, childcare and charitable assistance. And if empowered to, they could use the Church of England's considerable landholdings to build a new generation of almshouses tailored for residential social care.

Churches are just one form of charitable or mutual aid organisation. There are countless across the country that provide everything from high-quality childcare to community transport or social care services. The government should increase the tax reliefs available to non-profit organisations if they are substituting for state-provided services. At the same time, voluntary organisations that engage principally in advocacy rather than service provision should no longer be eligible for government support, so that resources are allocated specifically to groups delivering vital services.

But without doubt, the form of association in most need of assistance is the family. There is increasing evidence of a robust causal relationship between family breakdown and the expansion of the state. Philip Pilkington, for example, has presented evidence that shows welfare spending (exempting family transfer payments) would be almost 20 per cent lower if single parents were instead married; families are on average much less likely to depend on benefits than single parents. Family breakdown is a powerful driver of the mental health difficulties that are driving health-related benefits expenditure, and reduced care provision for those in old age through the family implies a requirement for greater provision via the state.[11]

Collapsing fertility rates also pose an immense challenge for our society. Unless we expand the number of young people in this country, an ageing population will necessitate higher levels of taxation to meet the demand for public services. We currently manage the situation by operating a remarkably lax immigration policy, thereby importing large volumes of human capital in particular to man our health and social care sectors.

Families are the surest example of the case made in this book; that by restoring those conditions which facilitate human flourishing, we can restore society to health, and that healthiness will be reflected in the dynamism of the economy. Families do not seek to nurture their children in order that they might participate successfully in the workforce. Nor do they care for their aged relatives in order to reduce their potential fiscal burden. They do these things out of love and an intimate sense of obligation. But the indirect, unintended consequence of healthy families is a stronger economy.

We need, as Pilkington argues, not a natalist policy but a *family* policy – one that promotes families as vital settings of support, moral education and belonging. This will involve a range of interventions. First, the tax code needs to be reformed so that it no longer penalises families and treats married couples as a single person for tax purposes. Family members who wish to care for elderly relatives should be able to draw cash-in-kind payments from the social care insurance policies advocated above. Similarly, as David Goodhart has recommended, the £9 billion the government currently spends subsidising nursery care should also be available as a cash payment for parents who choose to provide care at home. Finally, the child benefit cap should be reinstated, but a new tax allowance should be introduced which increases based on the number of children the family has.

For some time, politicians have shied away from assertively supporting traditional family structures for fear of appearing intolerant of single parents, or those who opt not to have children. Governments *must* generalise, however, and positively promote structures and institutions they deem to be in the interest of their people. It is entirely possible to do this while remaining tolerant and compassionate. In this case, families are an essential source of support and self-sufficiency, and the environment in which relationships vital for human flourishing can be built. There should be no qualms about encouraging them.

An End to Consumptionism

What would be required to transform our consumptionist economy into one motivated by investment and a concern for the long term? Some of the changes proposed above regarding the funding of welfare will help. But they will not suffice.

The tax system more generally needs to be rebalanced to support savings and investment. One serious intervention would be to levy capital gains tax on a sliding scale, such that the liability diminishes the longer an asset is owned. This will encourage long-term stakes in businesses, discourage extractive practices and incentivise investment in productivity. Dividends on shares in British companies could be exempt from tax to encourage pension funds in particular to invest in UK PLC. The VAT base should be widened and emptied of unjustifiable exemptions to create space for a reduction in direct taxes.

Further support for the family ought to be instituted too. Inheritance tax should be scrapped for any estate worth under £2 million, and as part of the wider move away from individual and towards household assessment for tax liability, a new family savings vehicle or ISA should be created with fully transferable savings allowances.

All of this will help improve the stock of resources flowing towards future generations. But it is not enough to simply boost savings. We also need to get those savings to the parts of the economy that badly need investment, and which will drive improvements in our productive capacity.

We do not need another 'industrial strategy', but rather a strategy for industry that seeks to make it more productive and profitable *in general*, creates a better environment for the private sector to make its own investment decisions, and *reduces* dependency on state intervention. There would be two main prongs to this approach: firstly, to improve investment in skills so we have a workforce that can support innovative and enterprising companies; and secondly, greater energy abundance, which will reduce input costs for *all* businesses.

On training, our ability to furnish businesses operating in Britain with a skilled workforce has been severely hampered by a political consensus advocating for a higher and higher proportion of our young people to go to university, even when this is increasingly not in their best interests. The state should not actively discourage people from going to university who wish to do so. But it is the case that our approach to post-secondary school education currently deters many people from taking non-university routes.

So many students are being failed because their university education is not a meaningful investment in their skills but a three-year consumption exercise funded by debt that will pose a heavy burden on them when earning. These are students who could actively be encouraged to undertake training in a vocation that would give them meaningful, dignified and reliable employment, but are discouraged from doing so by a culture which ascribes such status to a university degree, the value of which is increasingly contestable at many institutions.

We need a policy that promotes parity of esteem between different post-school educational pathways, including university and apprenticeships. This means ensuring that financial support mechanisms are equally accessible, regardless of the route a young person chooses. There should be a cap on the number of university degrees that are funded by the government annually, and money instead redirected towards technical qualifications and apprenticeships administered by colleges, employers or indeed universities who change their offering.

But the truly transformative policy that I want to argue for is the introduction of a child education savings scheme – similar to the abortive child trust funds advocated by the American scholar Bruce Ackerman and more tentatively by the Blair government. At birth, every child would receive a state-funded savings account, seeded with a small sum that earns investment returns. At age 18, the funds could be withdrawn tax-free, but only for approved educational or training purposes. To support fair access, particularly for children from lower-income households, a portion of existing child benefit payments could be automatically redirected into the savings account, with the option for families to top up contributions. Companies could support their employees with a matched contribution. This would not only encourage early investment in all forms of tertiary education – academic and vocational – but it could also over time replace student loans and thus reduce dependency on debt.

On energy, we need to strip away the compliance requirements that vastly inflate the cost of delivering new infrastructure. Most importantly, we need to stop expecting each infrastructure project to solve wider objectives surrounding the natural environment. These are important objectives, but they ought to be addressed separately. Not *every* new piece of infrastructure needs to improve the habitation of the UK's bat population.

We also need to simply stop 'banning' forms of investment.[12] We need to permit oil and gas exploration, and we need to expedite the delivery of grid infrastructure. As suggested above, we should expedite any new energy generation plant which comes with a community benefit agreement, like reduced bills within a given geographical proximity. Investing in energy abundance is probably the most direct way we can support the profitability of businesses, expand our productive capacity and put us in a position to reduce the current account deficit.

This package of reforms will help to lengthen people's time horizons in Britain and give many more households and businesses a stake in the multigenerational enterprise of improving our prosperity. But in the final analysis, ending our consumptionist economic model will require us to tackle one additional driver: we need a plan for turning off the tap of mass immigration, which not only serves as a major obstacle to the transition towards a higher investment economy, but is itself another source of that debilitating sense of disownership at the core of our social and economic malaise. Partly, improving the incentives to save and invest will reduce our dependency on imported labour. But that alone will not suffice. We also need to tackle mass immigration *directly*.

Sovereignty and Citizenship

The nation is the organic expression of our common identity. It is not imposed from above, but represents the sum of all of the interpersonal and inter-community relationships, both historic and contemporary, between people who call this place home. It creates a framework within which communities can thrive and the people of these islands can flourish. It enables us to see the problems of strangers in this country as *our* problems. It gives us all a sense of belonging and rootedness. And it stretches our time horizons, reminding us of obligations both to those who have gone before, as well as to those who will inherit this country in the future.

But the nation subsists on a feeling of ownership among its people. We call this sense of ownership *citizenship* – the idea that our membership of the national community comes with both advantages and obligations to others who belong to it. We have eroded that idea, and so the nation itself is beginning to disintegrate.

Reversing these trends requires citizenship to mean something again: a genuine balance of rights and responsibilities for those who wish to be a part of this country. That means interventions on both immigration and national integration.

Any form of community that relies on mutually shared burdens and benefits must have some form of control over its membership. That sense of solidarity and control, however, is dangerously undercut when a policy of immigration is followed which has no regard for the pace of change wrought on the community, nor the dispositions of those joining it. This is effectively the policy we have pursued to support high levels of consumptionism – high levels of immigration to keep the labour market loose and public sector labour costs low. But mass immigration along these lines without integration begets a sense of unfairness which undermines burden sharing and diminishes long-term thinking about society and the economy.

Our approach to immigration needs to be radically rethought, and there must necessarily be a quantitative dimension to this rethink. It is simply not possible to properly integrate as many as 1.3 million new people each year and treat those arriving with the dignity they deserve while simultaneously meeting the desire of those who already live here to see their national community conserved and maintained. At the same time, mass immigration props up an economic model that is inflicting significant harm on our society.

There should be an annual cap on annual immigration to the UK, set by Parliament, and with the object of reducing it over time to the tens of thousands. This will necessarily be a multi-year transition, as productivity improvements reduce the need for cheap labour. A visa auction system could be introduced to promote high-skilled immigration and shift incentives in both the public and private sectors.[13] The Graduate Visa route should be abolished, and those high-skilled overseas students who study in Britain should be encouraged to secure the right to remain in the country if they so wish. The immigration salary threshold should be raised and open-ended visa routes scrapped.

Even with these changes, the existing constitutional framework makes it immensely difficult for the government to remove individuals who break the law and enter the country *illegally*. That is why, as I have advocated, we must reconsider our membership of international treaties and cease the practice of asking courts to make what are intrinsically political decisions about border policy.

Most pressingly, the European Convention on Human Rights (ECHR), in combination with the Human Rights Act which incorporated the ECHR into domestic law, have effectively transferred control over UK borders to the European Court of Human Rights (ECtHR). Over time, innovations in case law have greatly expanded the 'protective reach' of the ECHR's provisions, and in so doing reduced the ability of the British state to prosecute the deportation of those individuals who are here illegally and often pose real risks to members of the community. In several cases, for example, the government has been prevented from deporting those who have committed violent crimes because they might face discrimination in their country of origin.[14]

These problems do not just afflict the UK. But renegotiating the Court's remit would require unanimous consent of every one of the forty-six members of the Council of Europe. It might be wiser for the government to work with allies with similar concerns about the ECtHR's jurisdiction to establish a reformed Court based upon an originalist interpretation of the Convention – one which ensures humanitarian obligations are met but which permits sovereign governments to remove individuals who commit crimes against its citizens.

If these efforts fail, the government should leave the ECHR. Our respect as a nation for inviolable basic rights and our humanitarian responsibilities to those around the world did not commence with the ECHR – indeed, many of its provisions were based on freedoms in British common law that have existed for centuries – and it would not end by leaving it. As part of this undertaking, the government would introduce proper routes for asylum seekers and establish a fixed number for annual admissions included in the overall immigration cap; these could be flexed in the case of a humanitarian disaster, for example, but remain subject to parliamentary control.

The government would also need to repeal or reform the Human Rights Act and return Britain to our common law tradition, which reconciles parliamentary sovereignty with a respect for individual rights. And finally, it would need to introduce an offshoring arrangement for the processing of individuals who enter the UK unlawfully from a safe country and not through the proper asylum routes. This would be best conducted on a British overseas territory like Ascension Island. Those with genuine asylum claims would be resettled in a safe country with which the UK has an agreement; those without – often economic migrants – would be either resettled in safe third countries or allowed to return to their home country.[15]

At the same time, we need to think far more concertedly about the qualitative aspects of our immigration system too. To some extent, the issues with scale are derivative; what makes mass immigration so objectionable is that its very magnitude prohibits us from paying attention to the character and human concerns of those who wish to enter our country. It treats newcomers instrumentally, and is indifferent to whether or not they are provided with the cultural resources to integrate properly, or the opportunities to become invested citizens of our country.

Multiculturalism is the clearest expression of this indifference. Often badged as its own form of respect for difference and human rights, it is in fact a radical example of apathy and relativism which leaves society less cohesive, communities less capable of peaceful coexistence, and people less able to flourish. Such a policy must be explicitly disavowed and replaced with a policy of pluralism – one that recognises human variety and the immense value it brings to society, but which is dedicated to the maintenance of a common cultural inheritance that galvanises communities to work together and transcend their differences.

First and foremost, all those entering the UK should be capable of speaking basic English subject to a test prior to immigrating, including dependants. Refugees entering the country would be provided free but compulsory lessons in English. Secondly, the government must devise a common history curriculum to be taught to students up until the age of 14. There have been discussions about a non-statutory curriculum, but this one should be placed on a statutory footing with appropriate flexibility for teachers. It should be knowledge-rich and designed explicitly to give our children a common set of reference points about the history of the nation to which they belong, and about which they can be proud. Support should also be given for the history and languages of Britain's constituent nations of England, Wales, Scotland and Northern Ireland.

It is entirely right that children have the opportunity to learn the history of other nations, or about events and episodes or trends that have an international salience rather than a narrow, national one. But this should not come at the expense of our young people having a proper understanding of the nation they belong to, or of the state's obligation to support the transmission across generations of a common cultural and historical inheritance.

As well as addressing the impression that newcomers are not embracing this country's language and culture, we also need to address the feeling that many who have moved to Britain are drawing significantly from the social safety net before they have contributed to it. The idea that non-British nationals are claiming around £1 billion in benefit payments every month is difficult for people to stomach when their tax burden is rising. Raising the salary threshold will go some way to reducing this problem, but further steps should be taken, including raising the immigration health surcharge and increasing the residency requirement before people become eligible for indefinite leave to remain – an immigration status that renders individuals eligible for a range of benefits.

Two final ideas should be considered for restoring cohesion and national solidarity. The first is radical: a scheme of national service. Unfortunately, what is a fundamentally laudable idea for improving the sense of responsibility and stake among our younger generations has been set back by it being floated as part of a fractious election campaign, and by the fact that young people face highly limited economic prospects in the present big state, high taxation status quo. Yes, we must teach our young people responsibility, but that ought to come with the opportunity of a more prosperous life too.

To this end, a scheme of national service should in the first instance be voluntary and competitive, and have a specific defence focus. Those turning 18 each year would be tested, and their eligibility for service recorded. There would be a selective element for those wishing to serve, and a limited number of places available, subsidised through savings on university subsidies. Service would last for two years, but the reward for successful completion would be an income tax deduction until the age of 35, or some similar inducement. The aim should be for at least 10,000 people to participate per annum. A selective programme such as this would give a valuable boost to the armed forces, and could be widened if necessary for our nation's defence. Eventually, it might become a mark of excellence to potential employers.

Finally, a concerted effort ought to be made to promote the preservation of the country's natural environment. A sense of *place*, as we examined earlier, is the other essential component of nationhood, and citizens ought to feel connected with the geography and landscape that previous generations have encountered and enjoyed. This is not simply a matter for rural communities either; city dwellers experience the same emotional connection and sense of reverence when they visit the English countryside, because it represents a common inheritance that we ought to nurture and pass on.

Much that I have recommended will involve permitting change and development which for too long has been prohibited by a state that is increasingly censorious, confiscatory and interventionist. But that ought to go alongside efforts to conserve and enhance those things of permanent value. Citizenship in this country is not simply about preserving the intangible aspects of our shared national inheritance. It also consists in taking ownership of the physical place we call home, and conserving it for future generations.

Conservationism has in many ways become hijacked by activists who are deeply hostile to the idea of personal responsibility, and are more committed to a radical, top-down version of environmentalism at the expense of local initiatives. This need not be the case, however. Conservationism has a basic affinity with conservatism, in its motivation to maintain and preserve, and in its scepticism of change for change's sake. Conservatives should reclaim conservationism, rearticulating it as a case for personal and local responsibility for the natural world. Indeed, they should set out the case for why radical environmentalism, with its top-down targets, heavy regulation and privileging of international initiatives is likely to make the ends they seek even more distant, because such an approach destroys the sense of home and love of place which is the true source of a desire to conserve.[16]

We should support community land trusts to take ownership of plots of treasured local green space, for which local people can be custodians. Nationally, initiatives should be launched to plant new forests and establish new national parks for the benefit of all. And finally, the government must recognise that the role of farmers in national life cannot be reduced to their 'Gross Value Added'. They are the guardians of our natural landscapes and the trustees of rural life, roles they are rightly proud of.

Those social functions are of immeasurable value, and we should recognise this by better funding the provision of public goods with public money, while reducing the immense regulatory burden – particularly that of a health and safety nature – which makes it impossible for small farms to operate. We need a conservation policy which avoids 'the tragedy of the commons' in which things that are treated as 'everyone's responsibility' in reality become nobody's responsibility. We need to give resources back to local people and foster their natural desire to preserve the place they call home.

Restoration

To the extent that they constitute discrete methods for promoting the values of ownership in Britain, politicians could cherry-pick particular proposals from above to instigate. But that is really to miss the wider change I am advocating for, which is to definitively reverse a cultural trend that has carried on uninterrupted since the mid-point of the last century.

From this perspective, the proposals I have made are interconnected: politicians cannot return powers to us that they have already given to other bodies, so restoring parliamentary government must happen before anything else. Diffuse private property is the material basis for a society of owners, but we shall need to create an economic environment that supports wealth creation and savings to make that diffusion possible. If we want to create the space for charities, mutuals, households and businesses to come up with their own solutions to the challenges of social provision, the state needs to draw less in taxation and give people the opportunity to choose what to do with their earnings. And if we want the wider obligations that are owed to people of the same nation to be sustainable in the long run, citizenship must mean a genuine balance of rights and responsibilities again.

For this to work – to genuinely restore a society in which the state plays a smaller role, and people have more space to flourish in their families and communities – the programme I'm advancing cannot be an afterthought or an optional extra. It must be the central and driving purpose not just for government, but for all of us.

Conclusion: Taking Ownership

> *I am quite aware that several of my contemporaries have thought that nations are never masters of themselves on this earth and that of necessity they obey some kind of insurmountable and senseless force which stems from past events, or from race, or from the soil, or from climate.*
>
> *Those are false and craven doctrines which can only be the product of feeble men or small-minded nations. Providence has created a human being neither wholly independent nor totally slavish. It has, true enough, drawn around each man a circle of fate from which he has no means of escaping but, within its broad boundaries, man is powerful and free, just like nations.*[1] – Alexis de Tocqueville

It seems to me that the most salient anxieties in our politics today concern a feeling that we have lost control of our lives in some way. There is a growing belief that Parliament no longer truly determines the laws we live by, that the police no longer command our streets, and that our economy is increasingly at the mercy of global forces – energy shocks, pandemics, market swings – that are beyond our influence. People feel that their communities are being reshaped – physically, culturally, demographically – without their input or consent. These are all symptoms of a deeper fear: that we are no longer in charge of our individual or collective destinies.

In response, many turn to the state. They hope that by expanding *its* power, they can somehow augment their *own*. If the state can insulate us from risk, they reason, it can offer a certainty – which appeals as a form of control itself. This mindset increasingly shapes how we approach economic policy: more regulation, more public spending, more intervention – all in the hope that providing the state with a firmer grip of the economy will produce better outcomes. It is a version of the argument that for a nation to be free and in control of its collective destiny, the individuals comprising it must be coerced.

But this is a mistaken belief. Uncertainty is not a defect of the human condition to be engineered away; it is its essence. A good politics does not promise to eliminate uncertainty, but to equip people to live with it well. Nor do we become more capable by expanding the state's reach indefinitely. On the contrary, doing so undermines the very sources of resilience and motivation – personal responsibility, moral agency, civic duty – that enable individuals and communities to face hardship and do good, as well as the vital impulses that underpin a dynamic economy.

This book proposes an entirely different response. Great nations are built not upon the strength of their governments, but on the strength of their people. Instead of placing even more responsibility into the hands of the state, I believe that we need to push the centre of gravity in our politics back downwards, towards the small, the personal, and the local. We need to give people *ownership* over their lives again, and to use the state to equip families and communities to shoulder the obligations of social existence decently.

I have argued that this is the most effective way to tackle the range of important societal and economic problems that our country presently faces. It is how we develop a proper approach to social care based on love and dignity, and how we make provision for our health and for our retirement without crippling the financial aspirations of the young and in work. It is how we increase the financial resilience of households, as well as the levels of investment in the economy. It is how we restore a sense of place and belonging within our communities, and generate the incentives for a more prosperous society.

But diffusing responsibility downwards is also intrinsically good; it is a project in giving people the chance to *choose* again, and without choice between different moral alternatives, we cannot fully develop as characters or flourish as human beings.

This is not a call for more liberalism, or more individualism. The case for ownership I've been making begins not with the 'rights' side of the political ledger, but with the responsibilities side. It is a call to duty, a demand that we return to an understanding of social obligations – to the weak, to the poor, to those who have gone before and those who are yet to come – as personal commissions that apply to us directly, not tasks that can be traded, or passed on to the impersonal state. It aims at the regeneration of that middle layer of social existence – the realm of small communities, of families and of neighbourhoods – by returning functions and responsibilities that have been assumed by the state back to civil society.

The ultimate test of good government today will not be how much power can be exercised from the centre, but how much agency and responsibility can be returned to the people of this country, and to what extent government can provide the cultural resources for them to exercise that responsibility effectively. This course of action does not promise greater certainty for the public. It does not seek to move our society to a place of greater safety. It offers something much more valuable: the opportunity for more people to have a real stake in their future. That sense of ownership has always been the source of our nation's success, in times of adversity as well as of peace and prosperity. It can be so again.

Acknowledgements

The ideas contained within these pages have been percolating in my mind for some time. But putting pen to paper did not become a real possibility until George Owers approached me about writing a book in 2024. I would first and foremost like to thank him and Polity Press for their encouragement and confidence in me. As a first-time author, I could not have asked for more.

I would also like to record my immense gratitude to the Pharos Foundation, without whose generosity I would not have been able to take the time out of work to research and write. I have greatly enjoyed being a part of the nascent intellectual community they have created, and for young writers like me, they are a vital source of support. My thanks also to my friend Bobby Vedral whose counsel I have valued immensely, the Mercatus Center, the Conservative Party Archives and Churchill College, Cambridge.

I have benefited from the advice and suggestions of a whole range of interlocutors over the writing period. They include Keir Bradwell, David Goodhart, Roger Bootle, Simon Clarke, Karl Williams, Munira Mirza, Michael Gove, Danny Kruger, James Orr, Tom Simpson, Nick Timothy, Lottie Moore, George

Barnes, James Cowling, Lizzie Hacking, Josh Smith, Sam Bidwell and Stephen Webb. Many read chapters and excerpts from the various draft versions, and their comments led to a much-improved final product. I am grateful to three anonymous reviewers as well, who vastly strengthened the contents of the book.

So many others have helped me distil and refine my ideas over recent years through debate and discussion. They include the team at Policy Exchange, the Conservative History Group, my friends and formerly colleagues at Civic Future, and my Dorset Council Conservative colleagues.

I also want to mention my dear friends in 37 Platoon, Dettingen Company, who I had the great privilege of commissioning with at Royal Military Academy Sandhurst in late 2025. Their example and dedication show that the desire for lives of responsibility remains strong among those coming of age in this country. They ought to be a cause for great optimism for our country.

Finally, of course, I want to thank my parents, who have been a constant source of support and guidance. It is to them that I owe everything, and to them that I dedicate this book.

Notes

Introduction: Poisoned Wells

1 Wilhelm Röpke, *A Humane Economy: The Social Framework of the Market Economy* (Wilmington, 2014) p.6.

2 Friedrich Hayek, *The Constitution of Liberty* (Abingdon, 1960) p.1.

3 See Tim Harford, *The Undercover Economist Strikes Back* (London, 2013) pp.1–13.

4 Torsten Bell, *Great Britain? How We Get Our Country Back* (London, 2025) pp.2, 71.

5 Evan Thomas, 'Attack from the Left: Paul Krugman's Poison Pen', *Newsweek*, 27 March 2009.

6 Mariana Mazzucato, *Mission Economy: A Moonshot Guide to Changing Capitalism* (London, 2021).

7 The Tony Blair Institute, *The Economic Case for Reimagining the State* (London, 2024) p.45.

8 Yoram Hazony, *Conservatism: A Rediscovery* (London, 2022) p.26; Edmund Burke, 'Speech before the House of Commons, 7th May 1782', in George Dearborn (ed), *The Works of Edmund Burke*, Vol.II (New York, 1836) p.469.

9 Röpke, *A Humane Economy*, p.125.

10 Pope John Paul II, 'Encyclical Letter, *Centesimus Annus*', 1 May 1991.

11 Irving Kristol, *Two Cheers for Capitalism* (New York, 1978) p.69.
12 Röpke, *A Humane Economy*, p.246.
13 Matthew Arnold, quoted in Roger Scruton, *How to Be a Conservative* (London, 2014) p.10.
14 Throughout, I distinguish between 'conservatism' as a political philosophy and Conservatism as the actions and attitudes of the Conservative Party proper.
15 Michael Oakeshott, *Rationalism in Politics and Other Essays* (New York, 1962) p.408.
16 Frank Meyer (ed), *What Is Conservatism?* (Wilmington, 2015) p.13.
17 Benjamin Disraeli, *Coningsby* (Oxford, 1982) p.87.
18 Roger Scruton, *Green Philosophy* (London, 2012) p.396.
19 C. S. Lewis, *Mere Christianity* (London, 2012) p.28.
20 Jon Moynihan, *Return to Growth: How to Fix the Economy, Vol.I* (London, 2024) pp.248–50.
21 David Hume, *A Treatise on Human Nature*, ed. L. A. Selby-Bigge (Oxford, 1896) pp.413–15.
22 Noel Skelton, 'Democracy Stabilised', *The Spectator*, 19 May 1923.

1 Diagnosis

1 Alexis de Tocqueville, *Democracy in America*, ed. Gerald Bevan and Isaac Kramnick (Bury St. Edmunds, 2003) p.817.
2 Edmund Burke, *Reflections on the Revolution in France* (London, 1988) p.373.
3 Gabriella Swirling, 'The Victims of Britain's Free Speech Crackdown', *The Telegraph*, 3 September 2025.
4 Moynihan, *Return to Growth*, pp.86–92.
5 Adam Smith, *The Theory of Moral Sentiments* (London, 2019).
6 Röpke, *A Humane Economy*, p.125.
7 John Paul II, 'Encyclical Letter, *Centesimus Annus*'.
8 Tom Holland, 'Humanism is a Heresy', *Unherd*, 26 November 2022.

9 Immanuel Kant, *Groundwork for the Metaphysics of Morals*, ed. Allen Wood (New York, 2002) pp.46–7.
10 See Alan Macfarlane, *The Origins of English Individualism: The Family, Property and Social Transition* (Oxford, 1978) pp.166–99.
11 Hayek, *Constitution of Liberty*, pp.50–1; Hugh Cecil, *Conservatism* (London, 1912) p.58.
12 See Aristotle, *Nicomachean Ethics*, ed. Robert Bartlett and Susan Collins (Chicago, 2012), especially Book I.
13 Pope John Paul II, 'Encyclical Letter, *Solicitudo Rei Socialis*', 30 December 1987.
14 Röpke, *A Humane Economy*, p.6.
15 Emmanuel Mounier, *Personalism* (Notre Dame, 1952) p.xxi.
16 John Paul II, 'Encyclical Letter, *Centesimus Annus*'.
17 Lewis, *Mere Christianity*. See Book IV, chapter six in particular.
18 Robert Nisbet, *The Sociological Tradition* (New York, 1966) p.47.
19 Peter Berger and Richard Neuhaus, *To Empower People: The Role of Mediating Structures in Public Policy* (Washington DC, 1977).
20 John Paul II, 'Encyclical Letter, *Centesimus Annus*'.
21 Mounier, *Personalism*, p.20.
22 Hazony, *Conservatism*, p.102.
23 Arthur Schopenhauer, *Parerga and Paralipomena, Volume II: Short philosophical Essays* (Cambridge, 2015) pp.651–2.
24 Kristol, *Two Cheers*, p.39.
25 James Vitali, 'The Property Owning Democracy', *Policy Exchange* (2023).
26 Noel Skelton, 'Problem and Principle', *The Spectator*, 12 May 1923.
27 Kristol, *Two Cheers*, p.39.
28 Max Weber, *The Protestant Ethic and the 'Spirit' of Capitalism* (London, 2022) pp.17, 23.
29 Alan Macfarlane, 'The Origins of English Individualism: Some Surprises', *Theory and Society*, Vol.6(2) (1978) pp.272–3.
30 Emmanuel Todd, *The Explanation of Ideology: Family Structures and Social Systems* (Oxford, 1985) p.108.

31 Samuel Smiles, *Self Help* (London, 1897) p.1.
32 Ibid., pp.1–3.
33 Roy Lewis and Angus Maude, *The English Middle Classes* (London, 1949) pp.277–8.
34 George Orwell, *The Lion and the Unicorn* (London, 1982) pp.38–46.
35 See Niall Ferguson, *Civilization: The West and the Rest* (New York, 2011); Deidre McCloskey, *The Bourgeois Virtues: Ethics for an Age of Commerce* (Chicago, 2006).
36 Röpke, *A Humane Economy*, p.125.
37 Oakeshott, *Rationalism in Politics*, pp.6–41; Hazony, *Conservatism*, pp.142–53.
38 Will Hutton, *This Time No Mistakes* (London, 2024) p.224.
39 Adam Ferguson, *An Essay on the History of Civil Society* (London, 1782).
40 Hayek, *Constitution of Liberty*, p.57.
41 Weber, *The Protestant Ethic*, pp.120–1.
42 Mustafa Suleyman, *The Coming Wave: AI, Power and the 21st Century's Greatest Dilemma* (London, 2024).
43 Hayek, *Individualism True and False* (Oxford, 1946).
44 Hazony, *Conservatism*, p.154.
45 Tocqueville, *Democracy in America*, p.589.
46 Patrick Deneen, *Why Liberalism Failed* (New Haven, 2019) pp.163–6.
47 Wilhelm Röpke, *Civitas Humana: A Humane Order of Society* (London, 1948) p.55.
48 Oakeshott, *Rationalism in Politics*, p.9.
49 Röpke, *Civitas Humana*, pp.31–2.
50 Oakeshott, *Rationalism in Politics*, pp.431–5; Hayek, *Constitution of Liberty*, p.227.
51 Burke, *Reflections*, p.151.
52 John Dalberg-Acton, 1st Baron Acton, 'The Roman Question', *The Rambler*, Vol.II, New Series (1860) p.146.
53 Karl Polanyi, *The Great Transformation: The Political and Economic Origins of Our Time* (London, 2024) p.161.

54 John Maynard Keynes, 'My Early Beliefs', in *The Collected Writings of John Maynard Keynes*, Vol.X (London, 1978) pp.433–51.
55 Hutton, *This Time No Mistakes*, pp.24–5, 243.
56 Richard Murphy, *The Joy of Tax* (London, 2015) p.59.
57 Torsten Bell, *Great Britain?*, p.71.
58 Tocqueville, *Democracy in America*, pp.805–6.
59 Robert Nisbet, *The Quest for Community* (Wilmington, 2014) pp.181–6.
60 Gus Carter, 'How Private Equity Ruined Britain', *The Spectator*, 26 July 2025.
61 Ibid.
62 Hilaire Belloc, *The Servile State* (London, 1912) pp.80–1.
63 Oakeshott, *Rationalism in Politics*, pp.371, 378.
64 Röpke, *A Humane Economy*, p.119.
65 Office for Budget Responsibility, *Fiscal Risks and Sustainability Report*, 2025.
66 Moynihan, *Return to Growth*, pp.58–9.
67 Matthew Parris, 'We Can't Afford a Taboo on Assisted Dying', *The Times*, 29 March 2024.
68 Szu Ping Chan and Tim Wallace, 'Reeves Warned Against "Jiggery-Pokery" to Plug Black Hole', *The Telegraph*, 7 August 2024.
69 Mariana Mazzucato, *The Entrepreneurial State: Debunking Public vs Private Myths* (New York, 2015) p.20.
70 Stephanie Kelton, *The Deficit Myth: How to Build a Better Economy* (London, 2021) p.24.
71 Aaron Teater, 'The Economics Behind Zack Polanski's Claims', *New Statesman*, 7 December 2025.
72 Martin Weiner, *English Culture and the Decline of the Industrial Spirit* (Cambridge, 1981).
73 Margaret Thatcher, 'The Moral Basis of a Free Society', *The Telegraph*, 16 May 1978; 'Speech to the General Assembly of the Church of Scotland', 21 May 1988.
74 Margaret Thatcher, 'Interview for Woman's Own', 23 September, 1987.

75 Alexander Rüstow, *Freedom and Domination* (Princeton, 1980) p.670.

2 What Is the State For?

1 George Will, *Statecraft as Soulcraft; What Government Does* (New York, 1983) p.144.
2 Oakeshott, *Rationalism in Politics*, pp.10–11.
3 Joshua Nevett, 'UK Facing Permanent Higher Taxes, IFS Think Tank Says', *BBC*, 29 September 2023.
4 Mazzucato, *Mission Economy*, p.23.
5 Tony Blair, *On Leadership: Lessons for the 21st Century* (London, 2024) p.146.
6 John Paul II, 'Encyclical Letter, *Centesimus Annus*'.
7 Mazzucato, *Mission Economy*, p.8.
8 Ibid., pp.60, 167.
9 Paul Collier, *The Future of Capitalism* (Milton Keynes, 2019) p.11.
10 Paul Smith, *Disraelian Conservatism and Social Reform* (London, 1967).
11 Ian Gilmour, *Inside Right: A Study of Conservatism* (London, 1977) p.152.
12 Roger Bootle, David Spencer, Ben Sweetman and James Vitali, 'The Costs of Crime – And How to Reduce Them', *Policy Exchange* (2025).
13 Danny Kruger, *Covenant: The New Politics of Home, Neighbourhood and Nation* (London, 2023) p.8.
14 Hugh Cecil, *Conservatism*, p.97.
15 John Paul II, 'Encyclical Letter, *Centesimus Annus*'.
16 Nisbet, *The Quest for Community*, pp.92–3.
17 Scruton, *Green Philosophy*, p.109–35.
18 Will, *Statecraft as Soulcraft*, p.144.
19 Kristol, *Two Cheers*, pp.127–8.
20 Adam Smith, quoted in Dugald Stewart, *Account of the Life and Writings of Adam Smith* (Cambridge, 1829) p.64.
21 Adam Smith, *An Inquiry Into the Nature and Causes of the Wealth of Nations* (London, 1852).

22 Hayek, *The Road to Serfdom* (Abingdon, 2001) p.78.
23 Ibid.
24 Michael Oakeshott, *The Politics of Faith and the Politics of Scepticism*, ed. Timothy Fuller (Avon, 1996) p.26.
25 Hayek, *Constitution of Liberty*, p.57.
26 Will, *Statecraft as Soulcraft*, p.156.
27 Ibid., pp.144, 151–2.
28 David Cameron, 'Speech on the Big Society', 23 May 2011.
29 Guy Dampier, 'Charities are Swapping Altruism for Activism', *The Spectator*, 25 January 2025.
30 Nisbet, *The Quest for Community*, p.251.
31 Kruger, *Covenant*, p.35.

3 The Property-Owning Democracy

1 Skelton, 'Problem and Principle'.
2 Aristotle, *Nicomachean Ethics*. See in particular Book I, chapter eight.
3 Aristotle, *Politics*, trans. C. D. C. Reeve (Indianapolis, 1998) p.120.
4 John Pocock, *The Machiavelli Moment: Florentine Political Thought and the Atlantic Republican Tradition* (Oxford, 2003).
5 Aristotle, *Politics*, p.28.
6 Burke, *Reflections*, p.140.
7 William James, *The Principles of Psychology* (London, 1890) p.188.
8 'Now, what is the fundamental principle of the feudal system, gentlemen? It is that the tenure of all property shall be the performance of its duties'. Benjamin Disraeli, *Selected Speeches*, ed. T. E. Kebbel (London, 1882) p.50.
9 Röpke, *Civitas Humana*, p.157.
10 Pope Leo XIII, 'Encyclical Letter, *Rerum Novarum*', 15 May 1891.
11 Ibid.
12 Ibid.
13 Ibid.
14 Ibid.
15 Hilaire Belloc, *Servile State*, pp.17, 57, 59.

16 Ibid., pp.84–5.
17 Ibid., p.43.
18 Skelton, 'Problem and Principle'.
19 Ibid.
20 Ibid.
21 Ibid.
22 Skelton, 'Democracy Stabilised'.
23 Vitali, 'The Property Owning Democracy'.
24 Samuel Watling and Anthony Breach, 'The Housebuilding Crisis: The UK's 4 Million Missing Homes', *Centre for Cities* (2023).
25 Jim Blagden and Sebastian Payne, 'Missing Millennials', *Onward* (2023).
26 Maximilian Bierbaum and Sheenam Singhal, 'Widening Retail Participation in Equity Markets', *New Financial* (2023).
27 This threshold, defined in the Companies Act 2006, changed in April 2025.
28 William Wright and James Thornhill, 'The Future of Smaller Company Capital Markets in the UK', *New Financial* (2024).
29 Thomas Piketty, *Capital in the Twenty-First Century* (London, 2014) p.481.
30 See for example Daron Acemoglu and James Robinson, 'The Rise and Decline of General Laws of Capitalism', *Journal of Economic Perspectives*, Vol.29(1) (2015) pp.3–28.
31 Jeff Larrimore, Richard Burkhauser, Gerald Auten and Philip Armour, 'Recent Trends in the US Top Income Shares in Tax Record Data', Working Paper 23007, *National Bureau of Economic Research* (2016); Michael Munger, 'Understanding Thomas Piketty's Capital in the 21st Century', *American Institute for Economic Research*, 15 January 2025.
32 Richard Murphy, *The Joy of Tax* (London, 2015) p.39.
33 Ibid., p.57.
34 Pope Pius XI, 'Encyclical Letter, *Quadragesimo Anno*', 15 May 1931.

4 Savings, Investment and the Intergenerational Contract

1 Burke, *Reflections*, pp.194–5.

2 Joseph Schumpeter, *Capitalism, Socialism and Democracy* (London, 1950) pp.160–1.

3 The term was first used by Samuel Strauss. 'Things Are in the Saddle', *The Atlantic*, November 1924.

4 Lionel Robbins, *An Essay on the Nature and Significance of Economic Science* (London, 1932) p.31.

5 Benedetto Croce, *Historical Materialism and the Economics of Karl Marx* (New York, 1914) p.172.

6 Hannah Arendt, 'Totalitarian Imperialism: Reflections on the Hungarian Revolution', *The Journal of Politics*, Vol.20(1) (1958) pp.5–43.

7 Smith, *Wealth of Nations*. See Book IV, chapter eight.

8 Ibid. Book II, chapter three.

9 Burke, *Reflections*, pp.194–5.

10 In economic theory, there is disagreement between those who endorse the classical, 'loanable funds' theory which ties investment to savings, and neo-Keynesians and modern monetary theorists who believe that investment is *created* by banks when they extend credit. Even the latter would have to concede that capital requirements introduce a financial constraint on bank lending. But even more generally, they would say that credit must be tied to real resources if it is not to be inflationary and destabilising. See, for example, the introduction to Stephanie Kelton, *The Deficit Myth: Modern Monetary Theory and How to Build a Better Economy* (London, 2020).

11 Nassau Senior, quoted in Edward Chancellor, *The Price of Time* (Milton Keynes, 2022) p.188.

12 Chancellor, *The Price of Time*, p.189.

13 Bank of England, 'Money Creation in the Modern Economy', *Quarterly Bulletin* (2014) p.14.

14 Murphy, *The Joy of Tax*, p.41.

15 Henry Hazlitt, *Economics in One Lesson* (Auburn, 1946) p.161.

16 Chancellor, *The Price of Time*, p.155.

17 Mark Carney, 'A Fine Balance: Speech Given to Mansion House', 20 June 2017.
18 Moynihan, *Return to Growth*, pp.58–9.
19 Wilhelm Röpke, *Two Essays*, ed. Johannes Overbeek (Lanham, 1987) pp.55–7.
20 See Robert Jenrick and Neil O'Brien, 'Taking Back Control', *Centre for Policy Studies* (2024); David Cowan and Tom Jones, 'Selecting the Best: Building a Future-Focused Immigration System', *Adam Smith Institute* (2024); Ed West, *The Diversity Illusion: What We Got Wrong about Immigration and How to Set It Right* (London, 2013) especially chapter four.
21 Migration Advisory Committee, 'MAC Annual Report', 13 December 2022.
22 Jenrick and O'Brien, *Taking Back Control*.
23 Moynihan, *Return to Growth*, p.177.
24 Tom Jones, 'The Follies of Human Quantitative Easing', *The Critic*, 29 April 2024.
25 Jenrick and O'Brien, *Taking Back Control*.
26 Schumpeter, *Capitalism, Socialism and Democracy*, pp.160–1.
27 Kelton, *The Deficit Myth*, pp.33–4, 242.
28 Ibid., pp.12, 89–90, 96.

5 Welfare, Healthcare and Social Care

1 Röpke, *Two Essays*, p.57.
2 William Beveridge, *Voluntary Action* (Abingdon, 2015) p.10.
3 See for example Jesse Norman, *Big Society: The Anatomy of New Politics* (Buckingham, 2010); Phillip Blond, *Red Tory* (London, 2010).
4 Bertrand de Jouvenal, *The Ethics of Redistribution* (Cambridge, 1951) pp.13–15.
5 Keith Joseph and Jonathan Sumption, *Inequality* (London, 1979) p.120.
6 Daniel Lilley and Ellen Pasternack, 'Balancing Taxes and Benefits: The Net Recipience Puzzle', *Civitas* (2025); See Moynihan, *Return to Growth*, p.107.

7 Moynihan, *Return to Growth*, p.92.
8 Röpke, *Two Essays*, p.62.
9 Nisbet, *The Quest for Community*, pp.130–40. See Jean-Jacques Rousseau, *The Social Contract and Discourses*, trans. George Cole (London, 1920).
10 Frederic Bastiat, *Selected Essays on Political Economy*, trans. Seymour Cain, ed. George Huszlar (New York, 1964) p.144.
11 John Paul II, 'Encyclical Letter, *Centesimus Annus*'.
12 Eduin Latimer, Freddie Pflanz and Tom Waters, 'Health-Related Benefit Claims Post-Pandemic: UK Trends and Global Context', *Institute for Fiscal Studies* (2024).
13 Jean-Andre Prager, Sean Phillips and Alexander Tait, 'For Whose Benefit?', *Policy Exchange* (2025).
14 Latimer, Pflanz and Waters, 'Health-Related Benefit Claims Post-Pandemic'.
15 Economic Affairs Committee, 'Oral Evidence: Economic Inactivity – Welfare and Long-Term Sickness', 29 October 2024.
16 Stephen Evans, 'The Benefit Trap', *Learning and Working Institute* (2025).
17 Centre for Social Justice, *How to Get Britain Working (and Pay the Bills)* (2025).
18 Jonathan Haidt and Greg Lukianoff, *The Coddling of the American Mind* (New York, 2018) p.27.
19 William Beveridge, *Social Insurance and Allied Services* (London, 1942) p.158.
20 Harry Eckstein, *The English Health Service* (Cambridge, MA, 1958).
21 Roger Bootle, Ben Ramanauskas and Ben Sweetman, 'The NHS – a Suitable Case for Treatment?', *Policy Exchange* (2025).
22 Parris, 'We Can't Afford a Taboo on Assisted Dying'.
23 Moynihan, *Return to Growth*, p.111.
24 Office for National Statistics, 'How Has Life Expectancy Changed Over Time?', 9 September 2015.

25 Office for Budget Responsibility, *Welfare Trends Report* (2014).
26 Danny Kruger, 'The Care Commitment: A New Model of Social Care for England', *Demos* (2021).
27 David Goodhart, *The Care Dilemma: Freedom, Family and Fertility* (London, 2024) pp.206–7.
28 Antonella Bancalari and Ben Zaranko, 'Adult Social Care in England: What Next?', *Institute for Fiscal Studies* (2024).
29 The King's Fund, 'Key Facts and Figures about Adult Social Care', 19 June 2025.
30 Beveridge, *Voluntary Action*, p.10.
31 Hayek, *Constitution of Liberty*, pp.225–6.
32 Winston Churchill, quoted in Peter Goldman, *Some Principles of Conservatism* (London, 1961).
33 Kristol, *Two Cheers*, pp.242–3.

6 People, Place and the First-Person Plural

1 Scruton, *How to Be a Conservative*, pp.24–5.
2 Lord Salisbury, 'Disintegration', in Paul Smith (ed), *Lord Salisbury On Politics* (Cambridge, 2010) p.342.
3 John Locke, *Two Treatises of Government*, ed. Peter Laslett (Cambridge, 2003) p.330.
4 Scruton, *How to Be a Conservative*, pp.204–5.
5 Roger Scruton, 'Brexit Will Give Us Back the Countryside, as Well as Our Country', *Spectator Life*, 29 November 2017.
6 Will, *Statecraft as Soulcraft*, p.24.
7 Burke, 'Speech before the House of Commons', p.469.
8 Orwell, *The Lion and the Unicorn*, p.37.
9 Michael Oakeshott, *On Human Conduct* (Oxford, 1975).
10 Hutton, *This Time No Mistakes*, p.226.
11 Roger Scruton, *England and the Need for Nations* (London, 2006) p.16.
12 Jonathan Haidt, *The Righteous Mind* (London, 2013).
13 Hazony, *The Virtue of Nationalism* (New York, 2023) p.53.
14 Hazony, *Conservatism*, pp.133–5.
15 Tom Simpson, *Trust: A Philosophical Study* (Oxford, 2023);

Christian Bjørnskov, 'The Political Economy of Trust', in Roger Congleton, Bernard Grofman and Stefan Voigt (ed), *The Oxford Handbook of Public Choice*, Vol.I, ed. (Oxford, 2019) pp.628–48.

16 Robert Putnam, *Bowling Alone* (New York, 2000) p.135.

17 Scruton, *How to Be a Conservative*, p.24.

18 David Willetts, *The Pinch* (London, 2011) p.6.

19 See Macfarlane, *The Origins of English Individualism*; Willetts, *The Pinch*, pp.1–23; and Emmanuel Todd, *The Explanation of Ideology*, p.108.

20 Scruton, *England and the Need for Nations*, pp.19–21.

21 David Goodhart, *The Road to Somewhere: The Populist Revolt and the Future of Politics* (London, 2017) p.15.

22 Phillipe Sands, 'We Are Citizens of the World – We Need a Global Passport', *The Guardian*, 25 August 2017.

23 George Monbiot, 'England, That Great Colonising Land, Has Itself Become a Colony', *The Guardian*, 17 February 2009.

24 Goodhart, *The Road to Somewhere*.

25 Eric Kaufmann, *Whiteshift: Populism, Immigration, and the Future of White Majorities* (London, 2018); Nick Timothy, *Remaking One Nation: The Future of Conservatism* (Cambridge, 2020).

26 Hutton, *This Time No Mistakes*, p.232.

27 G. M. Trevelyan, *History of England* (London, 1956) p. xxiii.

28 Ibid., p.1.

29 West, *The Diversity Illusion*, especially chapter one.

30 Karl Williams, 'A Migration Revolution', *Centre for Policy Studies* (2025).

31 Ibid.

32 Office for National Statistics, 'International Migration, England and Wales', 2 November 2022.

33 Paul Morland and Philip Pilkington, 'Migration, Stagnation, or Procreation: Quantifying the Demographic Trilemma', *ARC Research* (2024).

34 Scruton, *England and the Need for Nations*, pp.33–7.

35 Hutton, *This Time No Mistakes*, p.243.

36 Will, *Statecraft as Soulcraft*, pp.37–9.
37 Deneen, *Why Liberalism Failed*, p.89.
38 Robert Putnam, 'E Pluribus Unum: Diversity and Community in the Twenty-First Century', *Scandinavian Political Studies*, Vol.30(2) (2007) p.149.
39 Of course this is not to rule out universally valid truth, either. Conservatives are simply sceptical about our ability to have knowledge of the truth. Which is why they place their confidence in the stock of accumulated human wisdom embodied in traditions and institutions.
40 Rüstow, *Freedom and Domination*, p.448.
41 Röpke, *Civitas Humana*, p.133.
42 Deneen, *Why Liberalism Failed*, pp.72–7.
43 West, *The Diversity Illusion*, especially chapter four.
44 Wilhelm Röpke, *The Social Crisis of Our Time* (Chicago, 1950) p.10.
45 Jenrick and O'Brien, *Taking Back Control*.
46 Kruger, *Covenant*, pp.60, 81.
47 John Paul II, 'Encyclical Letter, *Centesimus Annus*'.
48 Scruton, *How to Be a Conservative*, p.ix.

7 What Is to Be Done?

1 Benjamin Disraeli, quotes in Samuel Smiles, *Self-Help* (London, 1897).
2 Nisbet, *The Quest for Community*, p.251.
3 Scruton, *Green Philosophy*, p.171.
4 Ibid.
5 Pete Burnham, quoted in Jake Anthony Scott, 'There is no Alternative? The Role of Depoliticisation in the Emergence of Populism', *Political Studies*, Vol.42(3) (2021) pp.325–39.
6 A policy that Nigel Lawson wished to instigate as Chancellor. *The View from Number Eleven* (London, 1992) p.819.
7 Employee Ownership Association, *People Powered Growth* (2023).
8 I acknowledge my intellectual debt to the late Frank Field and Andrew Forsey, who propose a somewhat different model in

'Revisiting Beveridge: A Benefits and Welfare System for the 21st Century', *Politeia* (2020).

9 Department for Work and Pensions, *Spring Statement: Health and Disability Benefit Reforms* (2025).

10 Prager, Phillips and Tait, *For Whose Benefit?*.

11 Philip Pilkington, 'Family Matters', *ARC Research* (2025).

12 Sam Bowman, Samuel Hughes and Ben Southwood, 'Foundations', 20 September 2024.

13 Stephen Webb, 'Why Is It So Hard Getting Immigration Numbers Down?', *Policy Exchange* (2024).

14 Ibid.

15 Policy Exchange, 'Stopping the Small Boats: a "Plan B"' (2022).

16 Scruton, *Green Philosophy*, pp.170–1.

Conclusion: Taking Ownership

1 De Tocqueville, *Democracy in America*, pp.821–2.

Index